चुप साधना

CHUP SADHANA

The Yoga of Silence

Mansoor

Edited by Clarissa

Chup Sadhana

www.chup-sadhana.com

yoga@chup-sadhana.com

© 2009 Mansoor

First published 2009
Revised edition 2009

Book design
www.sndesign.co.uk

ISBN 978-1-4092-5778-3

Printed in the United States of America
via Lulu Press (www.lulu.com)

Inspired by the talks of
Swami Ramsukhdas (1902–2005)
of Gita Bhawan, Rishikesh, India

and other teachers encountered on the way

CONTENTS

Foreword *9*

Introduction *13*

The Missing Link *19*

Not for Everybody *25*

How to practise Chup Sadhana *31*

Samskara, habits, bondage *39*

Shakti of Attention *45*

Content & Context *55*

Heart *63*

Self-enquiry *71*

Physical Yoga – Asanas *79*

Meditation, Dhyana, Samadhi *91*

Breath & Purification *97*

Bhakti Karma & Jnana Yoga *105*

Contraction & Expansion *117*

Prayer & Surrender *125*

Yoga of Happiness *131*

Boredom as an Opportunity *139*

Self, Guru & God *147*

Confusion of Ego & False Self *153*

Tapas – Walking through Fire *161*

Tattva *167*

FOREWORD

Mansoor was born into a traditional Muslim family in Old Delhi in 1954. Post-partition India was full of deep wounds and distrust between the different religious communities. From a very young age Mansoor was acutely aware of these immense contradictions and there was a feeling that somewhere, there must be a common ground and a meeting point beyond all these conflicting religious and sectarian beliefs.

In his teens Mansoor, by chance, started reading books by *Ramana Maharishi*, whose teachings were to later have a profound influence on him. At the age of 17, Mansoor travelled around Europe and went on to live in America for the next 24 years. There, he was able to view life from many different angles and explored a wide range of spiritual traditions: *Vedanta, J. Krishnamurti, Zen*, Catholicism, Transcendental Meditation, EST etc. He travelled on pilgrimages and at times was also actively involved with different spiritual organizations.

This period abroad, most importantly, led to and developed Mansoor's unorthodox understanding and appreciation of Indian philosophy. He had to explore outside, in order to recognize the great wisdom sitting in Indian spiritual traditions.

In 1992 Mansoor returned to India, discovered *Vipassana* and started practicing *Yoga* in the *Sivananda* tradition. A whole new path opened up for him, combining the practice of awareness learnt in *Vipassana* with *Hatha Yoga*. Mansoor became a *Yoga* teacher and has now been teaching and conducting retreats in USA, India and Europe for the last 13 years. His multi-facetted background and his openness to embrace and to experience Knowledge from many different sources, has given Mansoor a unique approach and he has stirred and motivated students from all over the world.

In 1998, Mansoor started studying the scriptures seriously and taught himself enough *Sanskrit* to be able to understand the original Indian texts. This knowledge of scripture, particularly the *Bhagavad Gita*, which has always been closest to his heart, balanced with personal experience, has given a depth to his understanding. Mansoor is able to share and communicate this understanding in a remarkable and revealing way, creating a bridge between the different traditions, East and West, ancient and present.

I have been very fortunate to have been working with Mansoor for the last nine years and to benefit from his guidance, his inspiration, and now to assist in writing this book on *Chup Sadhana.*

This book seems to have had a life of its own and has undergone many changes and transformations over the last 2 years. The final version, which has turned out to be an exploration of Silence, was written in *Rishikesh* on the banks of the *Ganga.*

Clarissa, 7 January 2009

आरुरुक्षोर्मुनेर्योगं कर्म कारणमुच्यते ।
योगारूढस्य तस्यैव शमः कारणमुच्यते ॥

Ārurukṣor muner yogaṁ karma kāraṇam ucyate
Yog'āruḍhasya tsay'aiva śamaḥ kāraṇam ucyate

Bhagavad Gita ch 6 verse 3

For one seeking to walk the path of Yoga, action is said to be the means. Action can take the form of formal or informal practices, to still the mind and reduce the mental baggage.

One who has started to experience the state of Yoga as the vast infinity of Silence, in which the individual self is no longer found. Abiding quietly as Silence is the practice.

INTRODUCTION

Chup means to become quiet and *Sadhana* means the practice. *Chup Sadhana* is the practice of becoming quiet, both inside and outside. Before one starts to talk there is Silence and after the words come to an end, there is Silence. *Chup Sadhana* is the practice of also feeling the Silence underlying the words, the Silence that supports sound.

We have all already practised *Chup Sadhana*. Before one learnt to talk, one knew how to be quiet effortlessly. Before one learnt to think, one knew how to be thoughtless. Before one knew how to be active, one knew how to be at rest. So the effortless state was and is always present.

Nothing new is being talked about. Just a new word is being used because over time, old words lose their power. The state of *Yoga*, *Samadhi*, Transcendence, Infinity, Timelessness, No Mind, are all synonyms for this Silence. Silence is also the closest way of describing an effortless practice. This Silence is not reached by effort, by practices, by striving, but is ever-present as the uncreated Subject.

To understand the principle behind effortless practices, the example of boiling water is helpful. Everywhere in the world, the nature of water is essentially coolness. When a pot of water is placed on a stove and starts to boil, it is no longer cool. The quality of the fire, which is heat, has entered the water. To restore the water to its natural state of coolness, all one has to do is to remove the pot from the stove. The heat will leave the water by itself. No effort is necessary.

Chup Sadhana or the *Yoga* of Silence, is the practice of experiencing one's Self, one's natural state, as the silent ground upon which all the experiences of life are playing.

It is a question of catching these glimpses of Silence that appear spontaneously in the gap between thoughts, between actions, between events, between the in-breath and out-breath and also when one is just at rest.

In Indian philosophy, the stream of thoughts is not considered to be unbroken. It is said that there is always a gap between two thoughts, even when it appears that there is none. In the same way as there is a gap between the frames of a film reel. When the reel moves through the projector at a certain speed, it appears that there is continuity and the gap is not seen. Similarly, the faster the mind moves, the less the gap between the thoughts is seen. The recognition of these gaps is the first part of the practice. Stabilizing and abiding in the gaps, is the next stage.

In these gaps one gets a glimpse of who one really is. Even to talk of getting a glimpse of one's Self is to create duality; it is not that there is one self that gets a glimpse of another self. Experientially, it is a feeling of coming together, of merging, of becoming whole. This, in the *Yoga Sutras of Patanjali*, is how the state of *Yoga* is described.

These states of spontaneous Silence have actually appeared in the lives of many people as some expanded peak experience, some incredible feeling that lasted a few minutes or a few hours. Somebody may have experienced this walking on a beach and felt as if a curtain had lifted, where they experienced themselves as being one with the wind, the waves and the sky. There may have been a feeling of the boundaries and definitions falling away. Another person may have felt being bathed in Silence, a feeling of being newborn or an overwhelming sense of purity. Someone may have experienced a sudden intense love for total strangers for no apparent reason, or a deep feeling of security. It could have been a feeling of all encompassing compassion for every living being, for every tree, for every plant, a deep sense of wonder or simply a profound rejoicing in being.

These examples are glimpses of this state of Silence, which underlies all experiences. It is that 'Nothing', in which all potentialities exist. This Silence is not the opposite of sound, rather that in which both sounds and Silence are appearing. In the early part of the practice it appears as an object to be gained, but later on is recognized to have been one's own Self, the Subject, all along.

The purpose of this book, is to link that which happens in the practice of *Chup Sadhana*, to what is described in other practices and traditions and to see, that behind the descriptions, there is a common understanding. The descriptions may be many, but what is being described is the Indescribable.

मत्तः परतरं नान्यत्किञ्चिदस्ति धनञ्जय।
मयि सर्वमिदं प्रोतं सूत्रे मणिगणा इव॥

Mattaḥ parataraṁ n'ānyat kiñcid asti Dhanañjaya
Mayi sarvam idaṁ protaṁ sūtre maṇi-gaṇā iva

Bhagavad Gita ch 7 verse 7

In the entire universe, there is nothing that surpasses 'I am', the one indivisible Self, present as the Source and support behind all the life forms and personalities.

This Presence is the continuity, connection and the enlivening principle behind everything. In the same way as the thread in the necklace, though not visible, keeps the gems together, maintaining the identity of the necklace.

THE MISSING LINK

When one reads the stories of saintly people, great people, who set out in search of understanding, or in whom Self-realization happened, one assumes that there was a certain goal that they pursued and reached. The descriptions can be so varied and seemingly contradictory, that it is hard to believe that only one understanding is being described. Naturally, one thinks that one of these descriptions must be the real thing and the others, distorted or half-truths. The one description that is accepted will depend upon one's culture, one's background or one's religious conditioning.

Some traditions declare that God is formless; some say that God has a form. Some declare that God is gained by devotion; some say that God is found by wisdom. Some say that God responds to certain names; some say that God is nameless. Some say that there is rebirth; some deny rebirth. Some declare that there is a heaven and hell; some say that these are states of mind. Some say that austerities and penance are important; some say only love is the way. In this way, there are endless discussions on the nature of Truth.

In fact, these different descriptions are not so important. What is important, is the understanding that has been reached about the nature of the seeker, the individual who sets out on this journey. The missing link, that connects all the practices, is the discovery of who the seeker really is and what happens to him when the goal is reached.

In most practices, it is assumed that the seeker is real and the doubt is on the goal. The doubts could be:

Am I pursuing the real goal?

Is there light at the end of this tunnel?

Will this path bring me any happiness?

Will I succeed on this path?

Would any other path be better?

Actually, if the doubt of the seeker were to be directed back onto himself, the practice would really take off. The seeker is Awareness, identified with a bundle of thoughts. These thoughts are the conditioning. Therefore, one can say that the seeker is nothing but conditioning. All the efforts, made by the conditioning, can only produce more conditioning. This is the built in flaw in all spiritual practices.

As the seeker walks the path, along the way, these thoughts, patterns and beliefs, start to unravel and the bundle falls apart. What is left is Awareness, without thoughts, and the individual disappears. There is nobody left. This 'Nobody' is the Impersonal expanded Self, that the seeker was searching for. The disappearance of the bundle of thoughts, which was the individual seeker, is the revelation of 'That'.

This is *Yoga* in the broadest sense. *Yoga,* in *Sanskrit,* means to unite, to join, to integrate. The part unites with the whole, the relative with the absolute, man with God. In reality, what is discovered is that a *Vi-yoga*, which means separation, never happened. Rather than two entities uniting, there is a realization that they never were disunited. The innumerable different practices of *Yoga* do not reveal the Truth, rather they break down this illusory separation between the individual and the Universal.

This Impersonal Self that is left over, does not reach the goal because it is the goal. It is 'That', from which all things come and into which all things disappear. It is that Fullness from which 'Nobody' has ever been separated. It is described as that state beyond duality, beyond coming and going, beyond losing and winning, in which nothing has ever happened. The individual seeker is the obstacle. The disappearance of this obstacle, is the answer. There are not two selves. There is no lower self that will find the higher self. That one self will hunt down and find the other Self, is the delusion. What drops away is the delusion. Self is always Self and never not Self. This is the missing link.

The intention behind this book, is to see how this missing link runs through different spiritual practices and traditions.

अवजानन्ति मां मूढा मानुषीं तनुमाश्रितम्।
परं भावमजानन्तो मम भूतमहेश्वरम्॥

Avajānanti mām mūḍhā mānuṣīm tanum āśritam
Param bhāvam ajānanto mama bhūta-mah'eśvaram

Bhagavad Gita ch 9 verse 11

When the mind becomes over loaded with baggage, the Awareness becomes cloudy and dull. This 'dullness' is unable to perceive it's Essence and the conviction, that 'I am' is a body, becomes entrenched.

The need of the body for comforts, the need of the mind for entertainment, and the need of the ego to survive at any cost, gets superimposed on this transcendent, all pervasive Lord of the Universe, present as one's innermost Self. This one delusion, is the cause behind all the other delusions.

NOT FOR EVERYBODY

In the frantic world of today many people may be interested in hearing about *Chup Sadhana*, however this practice is not for everybody.

Not for everybody, does not mean that any special qualifications or requirements are necessary. Many people are convinced that much effort is required and many conditions have to be met. The practice of *Chup Sadhana* seems so simple that people, who imagine the spiritual path to be arduous, may have a problem in taking it seriously.

It is said that when the *Buddha* became enlightened, for the first few days he sat around in a state of utter astonishment.

He saw that the understanding which had been gained, was so crystal clear and obvious. Nothing was hidden and there were no secrets. How could anything that was so present and so clear have been missed.

He also saw the futility of teaching this to anybody. In any individual where the instrument of attention had developed, the understanding would manifest spontaneously and no teaching was needed. If the awareness was strongly identified with the personality and the attention was covered with a lot of craving and aversion, all the teaching would be useless.

Later, he talked about a third category of people who had only 'a little dust in their eyes'. Where the instrument of attention was not completely ready but also not completely covered. These were people, in whom some preparation had already happened. They were ripe and had both the capacity and willingness to listen.

Similarly, *Chup Sadhana* may be of benefit to such people in whom some preparation has already taken place. Seekers can be divided into three categories.

The first is like wood that is wet. Wet means a lot of unresolved emotions, feelings, desires, conflicts that one is carrying. This kind of wood needs a lot of effort to ignite. There may be a need for many preliminary practices to dry out the wood, before trying to light the fire.

The second category is like wood that is already dry. Here, less effort is needed and skilful use of fire will have the wood burning in no time.

The third category is like gunpowder. Here, just a spark may be enough to get the fire blazing. Just a few words may be enough. Just a hint may be enough.

The following are some of the obstacles which tend to get in the way of the practice:

One difficulty is the inability to hear what is not logical. People from different religions, different sects, will often defend their beliefs and practices by showing the logic behind them. One tries to convince others that one's beliefs are scientific and make sense as opposed to other people's beliefs, which are not scientific and are nonsense. What is difficult to grasp, is that this state of Silence is not some special wisdom or great logic, rather it is a state of primordial emptiness. It is the answer to the question, 'what do you know when you know nothing?'

Another obstacle is the reaction to the use of the term 'effortless' practice. The individual seeker exists in time. In daily life, one makes effort today to enjoy the benefits tomorrow. Everything that one seeks, is gained by effort. When one brings this attitude, that works in the outer world, to the inner search, this becomes a major obstacle.

Some people may not know how to listen. There is listening and there is listening. Listening with the head, means either rejecting or accepting based on ones conditioning. Listening with the heart, feels like a confirmation because the heart already knows. Words, which come from the heart, can only be recognized by the heart.

Deep-rooted beliefs and labels coming from ones background or practices that one has done in the past, can be a major obstacle. What is needed, is the willingness to be in a state of not knowing. To look at a tree, without labelling it as a tree. To look at a husband or wife without labelling them. To look at anything, without knowing what it is, is a very powerful practice. To experience the Silence, without calling it Silence.

People who lead secretive lives, double lives, people who say one thing and do another, who have multiple intentions, who are confused and have difficulty with trusting others, will find the practice of *Chup Sadhana,* uninviting.

शनैः शनैरुपरमेद्बुद्ध्या धृतिगृहीतया ।
आत्मसंस्थं मनः कृत्वा न किञ्चिदपि चिन्तयेत् ॥

Śanaiḥ-śanair uparamed buddhyā dhṛti-gṛhītayā
Ātma-saṁsthaṁ manaḥ kṛtvā na kiñcid api cintayet

Bhagavad Gita ch 6 verse 25

Moment by moment, being aware of events and dramas of life, watching instead of reacting. As if watching from a helicopter. With patient determination, because it is not easy, in fact it will seem impossible in the early stages. Then shifting the attention to the heart, located in the middle of the chest, which is the place where Self is at home when one is at peace. This is the place of Silence, in which both sounds and silence are appearing.

Now, not thinking anything. Not thinking about God, about Silence, about Truth or anything else. Just being quiet and when thoughts arise, and they will arise, not trying to stop them. With the understanding that the thoughts are not coming, but rather going away, and purification is happening spontaneously.

HOW TO PRACTISE
CHUP SADHANA

One practices *Chup Sadhana* very simply, by just becoming quiet several times during the day for a few seconds. Just becoming quiet, just stopping. Let me see…

For example, one is talking and talking and then for five or ten seconds, one just stops talking. Just stopping and seeing what happens. No explanations. Or one is walking and one just stops for a few seconds, not for a long period, just allowing a short gap to occur and then seeing what happens. Or one is working and again just stops for a few seconds. In the beginning, even half a minute is a very long time, 5 or 10 seconds is enough. Then just observing.

Just seeing things as they are, without putting labels and if labels are being put involuntarily, being aware that labels are happening. The point is, that mental and physical actions are observed and this observing, is the Silence. Awareness of a sound is not a sound.

In the early stages *Chup Sadhana* may require a certain effort to reduce the noise in the head. Various practices, like *Yoga Asanas*, chanting mantras, prayers, going on pilgrimage, avoiding intoxicants, reducing the time spent in front of the television and radio, or not reading newspapers, can be very beneficial.

The example of a potter's wheel is helpful, in understanding what happens in the early days of the practice. A potter uses his foot to keep the wheel moving and uses his hands to mould the clay. If the potter were to stop pedalling, the wheel would not come to a stop straight away. The momentum that has built up, will slowly decrease and the wheel will eventually come to a halt.

Similarly, when one becomes quiet for 5 or 10 seconds, one may find that the 'creating of pots' does not stop immediately. One may find that the velocity of the thoughts has even increased. Here, the following understanding is very important: thoughts are not coming, rather they are going away. In the same way, the speed of the wheel is reducing by itself. Everything is going away by itself.

To practise *Chup Sadhana* means to rest as Presence with an understanding that whatever is appearing at the physical or mental level, is only appearing in this silent Awareness. In the beginning of the practice, it may seem that five seconds of Silence is no match for the vast immensity of noise. A moment of Silence may feel like a grain of sand on a huge beach. That is why, it may be difficult initially, to have faith in the effectiveness of *Chup Sadhana*. But once one starts, these short pauses of Silence will start to get longer. Within days, one may find an interesting energy or power building up. These moments of Silence may feel as if they are growing by themselves.

In everyday language, Silence appears to be like emptiness, like nothing, like a graveyard, like an escape from real living. This is just the problem of language. Silence is actually a highly charged state. Just like a fan that is moving at a very high speed, from a distance, may appear not to be moving at all. This Silence is full of life, it could not be more alive and its energy is finer than fine. It is quite a revelation to realize that this Silence is always present, in the gap between two thoughts, so intimately near.

If the *Chup Sadhana* practice makes one sleepy, then it is better to do some other practice that is more active, like *Kirtan*, *Japa* or *Mantra* practice. The point is not to sink into *Tamas* or laziness.

For those who have a devotional nature and a strong belief in the existence of God, *Chup Sadhana* can be practised by simply feeling God's Presence everywhere and becoming quiet.

Yo mām paśyati sarvatra sarvaṁ ca mai paśyati
Tasy'āham na praṇaśyāmi sa ca me na praṇaśyati

Bhagavad Gita ch 6 verse 30

He who sees God in all beings and sees all beings
in God, such a person is never away from God and
God is never away from such a person

A conviction that everything exists in God, and that there is nothing but God, with this feeling one just becomes quiet. Not thinking about God, not talking to God, just a feeling that whatever exists, is God. No questions, no answers, no explanations, no prayers. Just Presence, just Silence.

Another way to stay in this space is to notice the breath entering the nostril, touching the nostril during entry and watching the breath touching the nostril during the exhalation. Breath awareness is a very simple, easy and yet most profound way to practise *Chup Sadhana*. The breath is moving by itself all the time. All one does, instead of thinking that one is breathing, is to observe the simple effortless breath, without trying to modify it. Observing the natural breath, as it is.

The point is, that the silent inner State is already present. Due to non-stop talking, working, thinking, wishing, wanting, planning, it appears that the Silence is not there. These non-stop movements of the mind create a thick curtain, so to say, that obscures the light.

This is not a practice of 'doing', rather it is a practice of 'recognizing' what is already there. Even in ones day-to-day life, there are short periods when one is feeling peaceful, feeling at home, feeling an absence of craving and aversion. These moments are also moments of *Chup Sadhana*. That is why, it is good to recognize these moments when they appear.

As the practice continues, the gaps will expand by themselves. Eventually a point should come, when in spite of all kinds of activities taking place, the Silence is unbroken. In fact the Silence is always unbroken. Silence is Self and the Self is never absent. *Chup Sadhana* is also never absent. The food is already cooked and the dinner is served.

If one tries to hold on to the gap for a long period, a 'doer' as the holder of the gap will appear. This 'doer' is the product of the mind and inadvertently, the mental curtain will again be reinforced. That is why just stopping for a few seconds in the early days, is enough.

When one has been walking for a long time and gets tired, by taking a little rest, one finds the energy coming back. Actions do not restore energy, actions only use up energy. The deeper the rest, the more recharged one feels. The State of Silence is the Source of power. It is said that the most unimaginable powers possible, are present in Silence.

The practice does not create the Silence, it only reduces the content, which is noise. This is a very important point. Even when these peaceful states appear for a few seconds, they are extremely valuable. Just as one *rupee* is part of a million *rupees*, these silent moments are an integral part of the Infinite Silence.

The only true sign of progress in the inner path, is the increasing of this Silence. This yardstick is most powerful and clear. It cannot be misinterpreted, nor is it subjective as other yardsticks of love, compassion, wisdom, light etc. may be. There is no mistaking Silence when it happens, and also no mistaking when it disappears.

Allowing oneself to bathe in this Silence for longer periods, one feels an incredible sense of lightness and purity. All burdens seem to be removed. A feeling that one has absorbed all the profound qualities that one was seeking throughout life.

This Silence is not dependant on others, it is not dependant on a practice, it has no conditions. More importantly, this Silence is discovered to be ones own intrinsic nature. One does not get Silence, one comes to recognize that one is Silence.

पूर्वाभ्यासेन तेनैव ह्रियते ह्यवशोऽपि सः ।
जिज्ञासुरपि योगस्य शब्दब्रह्मातिवर्तते ॥

Purv'ābyāsena ten'aiva hriyate hy avaśo'pi saḥ
Jijñāsur api yogasya śabda-brahm'ātivartate

Bhagavad Gita ch 6 verse 44

The inner journey continues over many lifetimes. What has been gained in the practice in one lifetime is not lost, when that form comes to an end. It shows up again in the next birth, as positive Samskaras or strong tendencies, that propel one again towards the search for perfection.

This setting out on the inner journey is not so much a decision that an individual makes, rather it is a feeling of being pulled in that direction in spite of oneself. As if one is helpless and cannot do otherwise. Such a person with these strong Samskaras, may find profound results happening even from a somewhat casual approach to the practice.

SAMSKARA, HABITS, BONDAGE

The world is experienced through contact. Awareness as the Self moves out through the sense organs and the mind, to experience life. Creation is not possible without duality. Therefore all experiences take place in duality. During the experience the witnessing aspect tends to get lost and Awareness loses itself in the objects of experience. One forgets oneself as the Source. When there is pleasure, one reacts with craving, with a desire to have the pleasure again. When there is pain, one reacts with aversion and wants to push that experience away.

In Indian philosophy the result of every action leaves behind a certain impression in the mind, a certain residual energy. The actions and reactions may be over, but a little knot is left behind. An imprint is left behind. These knots or imprints are called *Samskaras*. These *Samskaras* live in the mind and act as seeds for new actions and reactions. The *Samskaras* may be positive or negative. These impressions in the mind do not come to an end with the death of the physical body, they continue to mould the consciousness after death and create the conditions for a new birth.

Samskaras are of three kinds. The first maybe compared to drawing a line on water. As the line is drawn, it also disappears. The second may be compared to drawing a line in sand. A line drawn in the morning may disappear by the evening. The third and dangerous *Samskara* is the line which is carved on a rock, using a hammer and a chisel. These are the *Samskaras* of deep trauma, deep anger, deep pain, deep craving.

Whatever one is doing in life, whatever the family or the society in which one is born, the kind of food and activities that one likes, the kind of temperament one has, the kind of unconscious drives and patterns, the seeking of higher knowledge or the search for sensual pleasures and finally the stream of thoughts that is moving through ones head every day, is the result of *Samskaras* from many lives and also from what just happened.

That is why different people doing the same practices may have very different results. Some people, who do not have a lot of *Samskaras* to work through, may experience very rapid results and others may have to struggle for a long time. That is why one should not compare one's practice and its results with that of another person.

Over time, these *Samskaras* of reacting with craving and aversion create deep grooves in the mind. These grooves are the patterns and the tendencies in which the mind gets trapped. This is the conditioning which one tries to come out of in the *Yoga* practice in order to experience one's original Silent State.

The purpose behind different practices is to generate the energy to eliminate these *Samskaras* present as seeds in the mind. As long as the seeds are active, they will continue to sprout and create new patterns and tendencies. In the heat generated by the practice these seeds are roasted and a roasted seed cannot germinate any more.

That is why it is said in India that the *Yoga* practice can transform not just ones body and mind, but also ones destiny. What one calls *Karma* or destiny is really these *Samskaras* in action. The Self, which is only unlimited, unconditioned Awareness, finds itself helplessly, as if without a choice pulled by these powerful tendencies. Freedom from these binding *Samskaras* is freedom from destiny.

It is not possible to go from a turbulent state of mind, full of negative, confused and angry thoughts, to a state free of thoughts. That is why *Chup Sadhana* as a practice is not meant for everybody. What is important is to first replace these negative *Samskaras* with positive ones. In every religion, in every practice, there is an ethical, moral preliminary stage to create a peaceful ground. This preparation is only a step to the next level. Many practices tend to get stuck at the level of positive thinking. One has to go from negative thoughts to positive thoughts to no thoughts

In the practices of *Bhakti Yoga*, *Jnana Yoga* and *Karma Yoga*, one creates strong new positive *Samskaras* to counteract the negative *Samskaras* that are pulling one down. In *Bhakti Yoga* or the *Yoga* of devotion for example, one develops a strong love for one's chosen ideal. This strong love and devotion then counters the effects of *Samskaras* of hatred, anger and judgement. In the practice of *Jnana Yoga*, new *Samskaras* of wisdom and understanding are generated to counter the *Samskaras* of delusion and unconsciousness. In the practice of *Karma Yoga* or consecrated action, one surrenders the fruits of one's actions. One starts to work for the happiness of others and new *Samskaras* of finding happiness in the happiness of others are formed.

In *Chup Sadhana* one does not struggle with these *Samskaras*. By just becoming quiet and not reacting, one becomes aware of the patterns and the energy hiding in them. In the beginning one may see only the gross aspect of the *Samskara*. As one watches patiently, resisting the temptation to escape or to justify, the deep memory behind it may become visible. This understanding of what the pattern is made of, makes the pattern fall apart. Like anything in the world, a pattern is also a composite of several threads. Taking the example of a piece of cloth, if the threads that make up the cloth are removed one by one, the cloth disappears by itself or is found to have never been anything other than threads. This effortless practice of purification, though in theory very simple, can be quite difficult.

न हि ज्ञानेन सदृशं पवित्रमिह विद्यते ।
तत्स्वयं योगसंसिद्ध: कालेनात्मनि विन्दति ॥

Na hi jñānena sadṛaśaṁ pavitram iha vidyate
Tat svayam yoga-saṁsiddaḥ kālen'ātmani vindati

Bhagavad Gita ch 4 verse 38

In the entire creation there is nothing more purifying than attention. This attention is the light of Consciousness, which reveals the world.

When one is befuddled, the attention gets fascinated by the forms. This is the experience of fragmentation. On turning inwards, attention starts to become aware of its intrinsic purity.

Abiding in the heart as attention is the perfection of Yoga, discovered in the course of the practice. The many different practices exist to bring the seeker to this understanding, just as all rivers finally end in the ocean.

THE SHAKTI OF ATTENTION

Nothing is more valuable than attention. Here the words Attention, Awareness, Consciousness and Presence are being used as synonyms for *Chup Sadhana*.

Whatever is done with attention becomes energized. Whatever one puts one's attention on, that area of life becomes enlivened. Similarly, withdrawing one's attention from any aspect of life, weakens that aspect and mistakes happen. Even directing one's attention on a plant, makes the plant flourish. Putting one's attention on the breath, just simple breath, makes the breath more harmonious. The breath becomes longer, deeper and more powerful, just with attention. Eating with attention on the chewing of the food, will change the entire digestive process. The change comes not just from chewing the food many times as doctors recommend, but also from the quality of attention that is directed on the chewing. The food in the mouth may start to feel so alive that it may seem as if one is eating that food for the first time.

In any action, the quality of attention is the main ingredient. When one has cooked with attention, the taste in the food will reflect that attention. There will be a feeling of something extra in the food even though it may be a simple dish. That is why mother's cooking is considered to be superior. When a mother cooks, there is love for the family in the act of cooking. This love and attention are actually the same thing.

In the practice of being present, a certain *Shakti*, or power wakes up. Awareness is not just some idea, rather it is a vibrant energy that enlivens both the mind and the body. This energy when it wakes up, seems complete in itself. Even to call it an energy is misleading because it is inseparable from one's core. It is one's silent Self.

An example is used in India to point towards this *Shakti*. When the long summer season is coming to an end, the heat is intense and people look to the sky hopefully for some sign of clouds indicating the arrival of the monsoon rains. At first, a few small white clouds may be seen and these clouds may come and go.

In time, darker clouds gather and eventually the sky becomes completely dark and full of moisture-laden clouds. Now one knows that rain is imminent.

Similarly when one starts to watch, true effortless Awareness only appears for a few seconds. These moments of being present lengthen and just like the presence of the clouds then become impossible to ignore. When the Awareness has become very strong, it is felt as a power and there is no mistaking it's Presence.

In the beginning when one is asked to be aware, there is a feeling 'what is the big deal' because the instrument has not yet been developed. It is like asking somebody to look at the night sky and observe the different stars and planets. In the beginning it may seem boring and after a minute or two one may lose interest because all the stars will appear more or less the same. Now, if one is given a high-powered telescope, one may be able to observe the stars more clearly and the watching will become very interesting. Each planet or star will appear unique. So it is with Awareness.

The comparison of the telescope and Awareness is just an example. A telescope is dead but Awareness is alive. Awareness reveals but also enlivens the objects of Awareness. It transforms what is being observed. The different practices that one does help to develop and fine-tune this instrument. The instrument is the Source and also the purpose of the practice. Awareness is the instrument, Awareness is the practice and Awareness is the goal.

Sometimes this *Shakti* wakes up spontaneously as a feeling of over-whelming clarity, a clarity of purpose, a lucidity in which the world is seen as sparkling and vibrant. It could happen in a cathartic moment of extreme danger, extreme anger or extreme shock. People sometimes talk about having watched themselves as if they were actors in a scene. As if they could see what they were going to say or do next. In these moments, it is the Presence or Awareness which has become the Subject. This Presence is the *Shakti*.

There are people who say that all the problems in the world can be traced to the lack of love. As one practises there is an understanding that attention is love. Then one sees that people seeking attention are actually seeking love. One sees this clearly in the case of small children, who are not getting attention from the parents. They will often find very destructive ways to get that attention.

One thing should be clear that here, what is being talked about is attention which is free of motive, free of craving and aversion. For many people this may seem like a strange idea because in day-to-day life, people always look with a purpose. There is a deep conditioning that one cannot look, or one should not look without a purpose. As the practice grows one can see, that attention and purpose are two separate things. Attention is who one is, pure Awareness in the heart. Purpose is whatever happens to be in the mind at that moment. For example, looking at someone with anger, that is also attention. However with this attention, the purpose also gets transmitted and creates a negative feeling in the person being looked at. To take another example, there is a pickpocket who is looking with great attention at a potential victim. The attention is pure Awareness mixed with the purpose of stealing. This attention will create nervousness in the one being looked at.

In many people there is a belief that love is desire. That to desire something means to love that thing. But this love is the opposite of hate and contains in it the seed of hatred. True attention is that Love, which is beyond love and hate. It is a purposeless Love. When one looks with attention, free of any intention, what gets communicated is Love. One can see this in the case of children when they are very little. They have not been told how to love and yet in their look one sees this uncreated Love.

This drive to get attention takes so many forms in life. Women will go to great lengths to look good because they understand the power in attention even better than men. Men will go out and buy a flashy sports car to get that same attention. As people get older, the amount of attention they receive gets less. Especially in modern societies where youth and good looks are given so much importance, older people start to feel like they are not there. People seem to look right through them. People in whom attention is very strong, are very present and tend to energize the environment around them. Everybody around them starts to feel a little bit richer, a little bit stronger, a little bit more confident. It is said that a good doctor is one, whose patients start to feel much better just by seeing him, or him seeing them.

The point is, that one is entirely made up of attention. In

fact one is the Source of attention. In all this externalized need for attention, the Awareness goes outward and the Source gets neglected. Through turning inwards, using whatever practices, the Source is re-discovered. Attention as the individual self, finds itself to have actually been the Source of attention all along. The personal self, in the search for love, discovers itself to have been that Source of love all along. This is the end of the practice.

In many traditions there is a practice of saying Grace, of blessing the food before eating. Here also, when attention is being brought to the food, the food takes on a different quality. When one enters a room that has just been cleaned, one will find a certain quality of light. This is not just a result of the physical cleaning but the attention that the one who was cleaning, has directed to different parts of the room.

When there is love between two people or a person and an object, the extent of the love is known by the amount of attention that one brings to that relationship. If one loves money, one is always thinking about money. This thinking about money and attention are all the same. When one loves a person, one is thinking about them all the time.

Once it is understood that attention is love, the practice of *Yoga* becomes crystal clear. 'I am' is attention, 'I am' is Awareness, 'I am' is the love that is activating the body and mind. 'I am' is the enlivening principle behind all activities. This attention or Awareness is in fact the only thing of real value in any person.

In all the perceptions through the five senses and the mind, it is attention that moves out as the perceiving power. When one looks at something, it actually means attention streams out through the eyes for that looking to happen. Similarly when one hears something, attention streams out through the ears for that hearing to happen. The endless chatter in the head is probably the biggest cause of depleted attention. Every thought, every emotion, every feeling, uses up some of this attention. With this clarity, one starts to protect the attention. When there is something of great value it is also guarded.

If one did nothing else in the spiritual practice except watching, no other practices would be needed. In the beginning, it is enough to just practise simple Awareness in day-to-day activities. Being aware of the body, of the breath. Being aware of the movement of the tongue while eating or talking. Being aware of the physical ear while hearing a sound. Being aware of the physical eye, while seeing different forms. Being aware of the feeling in the nose while smelling, being aware of the touch on the skin.

Eventually a stage may come when one becomes aware of a thought. One is able to be aware of the thought arising, staying and then dissolving. This is a great achievement. The realization that one is not ones' thoughts, rather one is that Silence in which thoughts are appearing, is *Chup Sadhana*.

यथाकाशस्थितो नित्यं वायुः सर्वत्रगो महान्।
तथा सर्वाणि भूतानि मत्स्थानीत्युपधारय॥

Yathākāśa-sthito nityaṁ vāyuḥ sarvatra-go mahān
Tathā sarvāni bhutāni mat-sthanī'ty upadhāraya

Bhagavad Gita ch 9 verse 6

Great winds in the form of thunderstorms, hurricanes, tornadoes, sandstorms, typhoons, all appear to be full of substance and power. However, the space in which they appear and disappear is pristine and empty and is unaffected by these great winds. The space is the same before the storms, after the storms and also during the storms.

In the same way, all beings are born in that Awareness, live in that Awareness and die in that Awareness, without affecting that Awareness in any way. All the dramas of birth and death, failure and success, war and peace, happen in 'That'.

CONTENT & CONTEXT

Awareness is the context, in which all experiences, internal and external are appearing. The experiences are constantly changing and are not steady even for one moment. The Consciousness or Awareness is the only thing that is not moving or changing. Bodies are changing, events are changing, experiences are changing, even the states of mind are changing but that, which is knowing these changes, is unchanging.

Resting as the context is the essence of *Chup Sadhana*. The Knower recognizes himself as that silent Space, in which these endless changes are playing. This silent Awareness is like the screen in a cinema, without which no movies are possible and yet, which is not affected by the quality of any movie. By definition, the screen must be neutral in order to reflect back all the colours. It must be without blemish, to reflect back the blemishes. It must be without preferences, to reflect back all the preferences.

Even though the screen is present in all the movies, during the movie it is not seen because the entire attention is on the content appearing on the screen and the screen as the context gets ignored.

Similarly, the Consciousness which is present in each and every experience and without which absolutely no experience is possible, is not given any value. It is considered to be nothing because it is not a thing and everybody is programmed not to give any value to 'nothing'.

In every experience, 'I am' as the Presence is so self-evident that what is there to say. The great saint, *Ramana Maharishi*, called all the studies of scriptures and techniques, 'learned ignorance' because the real purpose of all the scriptures is to know one's own Self. This is why one talks of pointing. Anything that one says about this silent Awareness becomes a quality and therefore more content. The context can only be pointed to, otherwise it will be reduced to an object.

What is important in all this is not, that content is better or context is better. In fact, because there is content, one talks of context. Because there is formless, one can talk of form. It is only when all the attention goes to the content, that the context seems to disappear and one starts to feel disconnected from one's Source. In the Indian way of looking, this is the real alienation.

A person may be living in society, have family members, many friends, many interactions, and yet still feel isolated and alienated deep down inside. On the other hand, a person may be living the life of a recluse with very few interactions and may feel a firm sense of being 'at home'. This inner disconnection with one's Source, which in modern societies has become the norm, is what is experienced as alienation. A feeling of being split from one's Self, a feeling of not knowing who one is, a feeling of being ill at ease in one's skin, a stranger to oneself. When one starts the inner journey, this connection with the Source can feel like a homecoming. Even though no visible changes have taken place, it may feel as if one is able to finally come to rest.

In India, the name of Gods and Goddesses are taken together: *Radha/Krishna*, *Sita/Ram*, *Siva/Shakti* etc. The male aspect symbolizes the Consciousness as context and the female principle symbolizes the creative process or what happens in the space of the context. The male principle, *Purusa*, is considered the witnessing Self, the non-doer, the actionless knowing principle.

The female is the ever active, constantly changing, never the same, creative principle, *Prakriti*. All this is a very mysterious dance beyond logic and reasoning, happening in everybody.

As in many other cultures, there is a tradition in India of concealing profound principles in parables and symbols. An example is that of *Krishna* as the divine flute–player and his relationship with the *Gopis*, the milkmaids of *Vrindavan*. There is a famous analogy of the *Rasa-Lila*, the ecstatic dance that takes place in the enchanted moonlight. In this dance, *Krishna* is standing in the middle playing his flute and the *Gopis* are dancing around him in a large circle. *Krishna* here represents the silent Consciousness and the flute is indicating that, that Consciousness is full of divine music. The *Gopis* represent the different situations and experiences that happen during life. All these experiences are happening in the presence of *Krishna* as the context or Consciousness.

In the second aspect of the dance, one sees the *Gopis* dancing in a wider circle and we see between every two *Gopis,* the form of *Krishna*. The circle is complete and in every gap *Krishna* is present. Every *Gopi* has a *Krishna* as her partner. Again, what is being pointed to is the empty space, the ecstatic Consciousness, present between two thoughts, two actions, two events.

In the practice of *Chup Sadhana*, Silence is the context. In this context the experiences of life, small or big, important or unimportant, pleasant or unpleasant are seen as appearing and disappearing continuously. Silence is seen as the unchanging space which is supporting all these experiences.

To take another example, throughout the day one eats different kinds of food, which may be sweet, salty, spicy etc. The question is, 'what is the taste of the tongue that is knowing all these different tastes?' People are always happy to discuss the different flavours and types of food. Hardly ever does one find two people talking about the importance of the tongue. It is the tastelessness of the tongue that allows all the different tastes to be experienced. Here tongue is the 'context' and the different things one eats in life are the 'content'.

Going a little deeper, one will find a Presence which is knowing what the tongue is tasting. This Presence is a neutral energy which is knowing what the eyes are seeing, what the ears are hearing and even what the mind is thinking. In India this Presence is pointed to using the example of the sun. When the sun rises in the morning, just the presence of the sun triggers countless activities and effects on the earth. Night turns to day, the air warms up, birds wake up, people get up, children go to school, people go to work etc. The point is, that the sun has not 'done' anything. The sun is actionless. It is only being the sun and by its very presence, everything happens.

This normal, ordinary day-to-day Awareness that is self-evident in all our actions, is the context. Abiding as this Awareness, for short periods, is *Chup Sadhana*. The main reason that this Awareness is not recognized, is because it is not an 'object' to be recognized. It is the ever-present Subject. One spends one's whole life searching all over for the extraordinary, when in fact, one's own Self is the most extraordinary of all.

ईश्वरः सर्वभूतानां हृद्देशेऽर्जुन तिष्ठति ।
भ्रामयन्सर्वभूतानि यन्त्रारूढानि मायया ॥

Iśvaraḥ sarva-bhūtānāṁ hṛd-deśe'rjuna tiṣṭhati
Bhrāmayan sarva-bhūtāni yantr'ārūḍhāni māyayā

Bhagavad Gita ch 18 verse 61

God that people worship, the Master of choices, dwells in the hearts of all beings as the personal self. With the power of delusion, this Master magician creates and dissolves all the different realities and sitting in the heart as the Enjoyer, experiences this merry-go-round of life.

THE HEART

Talking about the heart brings up confusion. In day-to-day life, we hear expressions like 'what is in your heart', 'what does your heart say', 'my heart is not in it', 'my heart is troubled', 'a heavy heart', 'the heart of the matter', 'heartless' etc. Most of us walk around with a feeling that the heart is like a vague emotion or words of a song. Others may think of the heart just as a physical organ.

From the perspective of inner practice, heart can be said to be the place where the form meets the formless. The junction point where the formless, as silent Awareness, connects with whatever the form happens to be: man, woman, child, old, young, good, bad, ugly, beautiful etc. The formless is the enlivening principle behind both body and mind. The body is alive because of the formless, the mind is active because of the formless.

When a person is beautiful, wise, radiant, incredibly talented, or very dear to us, in fact what is dear to us is the formless expressing through that person. One finds that when the formless has exited the body, the dead body becomes an object of fear. Experiencing oneself as that silent formless Awareness is the practice of *Chup Sadhana*.

Hṛdaye citta samvit

Yoga Sutras of Patanjali ch 3 aphorism 34

When the attention is in the heart,
whatever is in the mind becomes known

Attention in the heart removes the confusion in the head. The mind operates through the principle of thinking and doubting. The original thought arises in the heart, not in the head. The original thought is not in duality. It is only when it goes into the head, that it multiplies. The one thought in the heart, becomes a hundred thoughts in the head. In the head, this Awareness becomes the individualized ego self and all the files in the mental filing system become part of this personal self.

Bringing the attention to the heart, the true Source of happiness is found. Attention provides the power supply that keeps the activity in the head going. By moving the attention to the heart, the power supply to the head gets cut off. Instead of trying to stop the 'monkey mind' one just shifts the attention to the heart.

By bringing the Awareness back to the heart, the mental desire is offered back to the Source. Letting go, surrender happens when the desire comes back to the heart, back to its Source. The purpose of all desires is to find fulfilment. If fulfilment is present in one's Source then desires that take one away from the Source, are taking one away from fulfilment. In fact, desire is the only obstruction to finding happiness.

The place in the middle of the chest, to which one intuitively points when referring to oneself, is said to be the space of the heart and not the physical heart which is the muscle on the left side. The difficulty in talking about the heart, is that by localizing it to a particular place one gets caught in a half-truth. The heart, as Awareness, is also that which envelops the entire creation and out of which the entire creation appears. These two statements, the heart is in me and I am in the heart, cannot be logically reconciled. There is Awareness in me, this is easy to accept but I am in Awareness, what to do with that.

There is an example in *Vedanta* that is used to illustrate this point. There is space in a pot and the pot exists in space. The space in the pot is real and has its purpose and the space in which the pot exists is also real. Behind both statements there is a single reality. There is only one space. Those who have experienced deep levels of understanding, at this stage, become quiet. Only the heart can know what is the heart. Trying to grasp what is the heart with the head, only brings distortion.

In the practice of *Chup Sadhana*, when there is a willingness to be quiet, automatically the Awareness shifts to the heart. This shifting into the heart, makes the world feel like a different place. People may express this experience with different metaphors. Somebody may say that they felt 'touched by the hand of God'. Somebody may say that they felt 'the presence of God in everything'. Another may say that 'God was the air that they were breathing', one may feel extreme love for everybody and everything, a desire to embrace the trees or to kiss the ground. It could be a feeling of complete security and safety, a feeling that the world is full of light or made of light.

Sometimes we come across graphic images of the Sacred Heart of Jesus or in India we may see *Hanuman*, the monkey God, tearing open his chest, to reveal *Sita* and *Ram* sitting inside his heart. When one looks differently into these metaphors, it becomes clear that this Sacred Heart, this Christ Consciousness, is present in everybody as Silent Witnessing. This Sacred Heart is not limited to a place or a person but is that Impersonal Awareness, in the light of which the whole universe is perceived.

In one of the *Upanishads* it is said, that there is a 'sky in the heart' called *'Hridakash'*, in which the physical space of the universe is appearing. This *Hridakash* is Awareness or Infinite Expansion. This is the space of Consciousness in which the universe is perceived. If one were to become unconscious, the universe would disappear. This understanding, 'I am not in the world, rather the world is appearing in I am', is wisdom.

 Only when this Awareness is identified with the body, it appears to become individual and petty and then does not seem sacred any more. The important point is, that the individual awareness is the Universal Awareness. The space in all the hundreds of millions of rooms in this world, is only one space. Only the presence of the four walls creates the illusion that the space in one room is different from the space in another.

The individualized ego that is born out of body identification, is not a calamity. It is not that something bad has happened, that needs to be fixed. Body identification is necessary to get work done because the drama of life cannot happen without individuality. Just as in a theatre, a play cannot be performed unless each actor is able to enter the role that they have been assigned. This is the Indian concept of *'Leela'*. *'Leela'* means a play, a divine play. Nothing bad has ever happened. There is no original sin and there is no salvation or redemption. It is a game in which there is only one 'Player' sitting in the hearts of everybody, as Awareness. Both bondage and liberation happen by the Grace of the 'One' living in the heart.

This understanding is the practice of *Chup Sadhana*, just be quiet, relax and enjoy the show.

अहमात्मा गुडाकेश सर्वभूताशयस्थित: ।
अहमादिश्च मध्यं च भूतानामन्त एव च ॥

Aham ātmā Gudākeśa sarva-bhūt'āśaya-sthitaḥ
Aham ādiś ca madhyaṁ ca bhūtānām anta eva ca

Bhagavad Gita ch 10 verse 20

The Self, the Source, Brahman, the highest indivisible Truth resides in every being as the individual self. The Self in myself, yourself, himself and herself, is 'That'. This ocean of Bliss and Truth could not be any nearer to the one who is seeking it is the seeker.

This Presence is the beginning, middle and end of all beings. The entire universe is appearing in 'That'. Before anything happened, Self was full, while events are happening Self is full and when everything comes to an end, Self does not lose its fullness.

SELF-INQUIRY

Answers are not important but a really good question can save one's life. That question, which brings an end to all questions, is what is meant by *Atma Vichara* or Self-inquiry. *Atma Vichara* also belongs to the category of *Sahaja Sadhana* or effortless practice.

One of the greatest saints of India, *Ramana Maharishi* (1879-1950), experienced his awakening spontaneously around the age of sixteen. As related by him, one day sitting alone in his room, he developed a sudden fear of death for no apparent reason. He was a perfectly healthy, normal sixteen-year old schoolboy with no inclination towards spiritual life, philosophies or anything else of an esoteric nature. There was no reason to account for this sudden fear of death. He just felt that he was going to die and began thinking what to do about it. It did not occur to him to consult a doctor or his elders. He just felt that he had to solve the problem himself, there and then.

The shock of the fear of death drove his mind inwards and he said to himself mentally, 'Now death has come, what does it mean?' 'What is it that is dying? As he lay on the floor, he dramatized the feeling of the body dying by becoming stiff and holding his breath.

In that feeling of an inert body, he felt the full force of his Being. The Being that cannot be touched by death. All this flashed through him vividly as a living truth, almost without a thought process. He could feel this 'I' feeling as something very real, in fact the only real thing in his present state. All the conscious activity of the body and mind were connected to and centred in this 'I' feeling in the heart. From that day on, 'I' or Self was focussed on itself by a powerful fascination. This absorption in the Self continued unbroken. Other thoughts would come and go, like various notes of music but the 'I' feeling continued like a fundamental note that blended with all the other notes. Whether he was engaged in talking, reading or anything else, 'I' was still centred on 'I'.

The theory behind the practice of Self-inquiry is that when the question is asked, 'who am I' in relation to any event, the very asking of the question takes one to the Source of this 'I' feeling, the Awareness in the heart. In the heart, no personal individual self is found. What remains is impersonal Awareness without any boundaries. A feeling of being the 'Attention' that is free and complete in Itself. One can say that the inquiring self that asked the question, 'who am I' dissolves into this Infinity, or expands into this Infinity.

The answer to the question, 'who am I' is not an answer as such. The appearance of one's true nature as Silence, is the answer. Therefore no answer, is the answer. For example, one is knocking on the door of a friend while calling out to him. When the person opens the door, he does not have to say that he is there, his very presence is the answer.

The story of the tenth man illustrates the principle behind Self-inquiry. Ten simple farmers from a village set out on a pilgrimage to a nearby shrine. On the way they had to cross a substantial river. When they reached the other side of the river, one of them suggested that they count themselves to make sure that all of them had crossed over safely. He started to count everybody and counted only nine men. Having forgotten to count himself, he assumed that one of the group had drowned.

Another member of the party offered to re-count, in case the first one had counted incorrectly. He made the same mistake of not counting himself and also found there to be only nine people.

Now being convinced that one of them had drowned, the entire group started to cry with grief. A stranger who was passing that way, came over to enquire about the reason for the grief. On being told the story, the stranger immediately saw what the problem was. He picked up a stick and said, 'each time I hit one of you with this stick, you will call out a number, the first will start with one'. When the last person that he hit with the stick called out, 'ten', there was astonishment in the group and then great jubilation, great happiness on having found the 'tenth man'. Obviously, the 'tenth man', who was found had never been lost in the first place.

By not counting oneself, by not being aware of Self which is always present in all experiences, there is a feeling of dissatisfaction, a feeling that something is missing. The practice of Self-inquiry reveals this missing person, the missing Self to have been present all along.

For all its simplicity, this practice is probably the most sophisticated and profound means to dissolve 'the ego' . 'The ego' here is being dissolved not by adding new concepts or seeking answers. It is a process of intelligent, wide-awake Self-inquiry.

There maybe many concerns and issues in one's life. Behind these many issues there seems to be an individual who has the issues. This individual 'I' is the common denominator. This 'I' thought is like a bubble that appears in the ocean. In fact, it is not separate from the ocean. That is why, on seeking the source of the 'I' thought, the ocean is found.

After the first 'I' thought, the second thought is said to be the 'you' thought and then 'he', 'she', 'they', 'them' follow. When a personal 'I' is not found, miraculously the second person 'you' is also not found and the third person, 'he', 'she', 'they', 'them' all disappear. In other words, when one looks at the world as an individual 'ego self', one only sees 'ego selves' in everybody else. And when one looks as 'nobody', one sees the same 'nobody' in everybody.

The greatness of this practice is that this question 'who am I' can be asked in every situation in life. One may be feeling angry, bored, confused, fearful, greedy or happy etc. For example one is feeling unhappy. First, there is an acknowledgment of that mental state and then instead of wallowing in the unhappiness, one asks the question, 'who is unhappy'? If the answer is 'I am unhappy', then the next question follows 'who is this me' or 'who am I'. This question will then naturally bring the attention to the Source, to the unconditioned Consciousness in the heart.

Instead of removing the unhappiness by Self-inquiry, the one who was feeling unhappy is exposed. The theory is, that the thinker and the thought arise simultaneously and are inter-dependant. When the thinker disappears, the thought loses its support and also disappears.

The phantom self, the personal 'I', can be experienced as a constant dialogue and discussion in the head. Even though it seems that there are many people talking to each other in one's head, actually there is only one tape-recorder. This tape-recorder is a master artist and is able to mimic all the different voices. This is the 'false self' and on enquiring, 'whose thoughts are these' and if these are my thoughts, 'who am I'. The impostor in the head cannot remain.

Otherwise one may go through an entire lifetime, somehow believing oneself to be this insane dialogue in the head. One may spend a lifetime trying to resolve the concerns of the voice in the head and in the end only find exhaustion. By the practice of Self-inquiry, the very basis, the very identity of the 'ego self' is discovered to have been a phantom.

Self-inquiry removes the illusion of a personal self and reveals the boundless Silence present as one's own Self. Resting in this Silence is *Chup Sadhana.*

All religions, all practices declare that in the end, the ego self finally has to be confronted. *Ramana Maharishi* said that making the last question, the first question is the way of coming directly to the point.

तं विद्याद्दुः खसंयोगवियोगं योगसञ्ज्ञितम्।
स निश्चयेन योक्तव्यो योगोऽनिर्विण्णचेतसा ॥

Taṁ vidyād duḥkha-saṁyoga viyogaṁ yoga-samjñitam
Sa niścayena yoktavyo yogo'nirviṇṇa-cetasā

Bhagavad Gita ch 6 verse 23

Of all the practices that are being called Yoga, only that which separates one's contact with pain or takes one out of suffering, can really be called Yoga. This ending of contact with pain can also be called a realization that a contact was never there.

This path of de-hypnotization will succeed if there is a strong conviction that it is time to wake up. Along the way, there will be many temptations that will pull one back into identifying with pain. Staying aware, while the buttons are being pushed, is very helpful.

PHYSICAL YOGA, ASANAS

For every state of mind there is a corresponding physical expression. Experiences in the body also create changes in the mind. The flow of body and mind is so intimately interwoven, that one cannot actually say that the two are separate. Every thought or feeling in the mind, is experienced in the body. Without a body the mind cannot experience. This is the simplest understanding of the physical aspect of *Yoga* practice.

There are seven *Chakras* (or six according to certain scriptures) through which Consciousness expresses itself in the body. In Yoga philosophy it is said, whatever happens at the physical or mental level, is in some way related to one of the *Chakras*. These *Chakras* are not in the physical body but rather in the subtle body. There are said to be 72,000 channels called *Nadis*, originating from just below the navel, which carry this vital energy known as *Prana* (or *Chi* in Chinese) and distribute it throughout the body. The *Chakras* represent the six junction points located in the region of the spine, where the main energy channels intersect.

In the practice of *Yoga Asanas*, one learns to shift the *Prana* from the lower *Chakras* into the higher *Chakras* thereby creating a shift in Consciousness. Each of these *Chakras* is connected to one of the five elements and one of the five sense organs. The sixth *Chakra* is called the *Ajna Chakra* and is the command centre located in the middle of the forehead. In the lower *Chakras*, consciousness vibrates at a lower frequency. Here the energy is dense and is mainly needed for the activities of physical survival. In the higher *Chakras*, consciousness manifests at a high frequency and the space becomes very refined.

When the higher *Chakras* have not opened, understanding is very dull and even the highest knowledge will not be grasped or will be misunderstood. If the higher *Chakras* have opened, everything starts to look crystal clear and understanding happens even without explanations. In this way, *Yoga* becomes a way to prepare the physical body for the descent of Knowledge.

There are hundreds of ways to approach the *Yoga* practice,

but broadly speaking there are only two things that happen. One, is the rising of the *Kundalini* energy from the root *Chakra* to the crown of the head. This is also called the sublimation of sexual energy.

The other, is what is meant by the word *'Hatha'* in *Hatha Yoga*. *'Ha'* refers to the sun channel called the *Pingala nadi*, running along the right side of the spine from the root *Chakra* to the point between the eyebrows. *'Tha'* refers to the *Ida nadi* or the moon channel, running along the left side of the spinal column. These two channels represent the fundamental polarity in everybody: the male/female, *Yin/Yang*, day/night, hard/soft, birth/death, the sympathetic and parasympathetic nervous systems, introversion/extroversion and *Prana*/Consciousness.

It is said in the scriptures, when these two channels become exactly equal or reach a stage of perfect balance, the third channel the *Sushumna nadi* which runs directly through the middle of the spine gets activated and transcendence happens. The rising of the *Kundalini* energy and the activation of the *Sushumna* channel are actually the same event. That means, without the balancing of the left and the right hemispheres, the state beyond duality cannot be reached.

The right nostril and the left nostril are the external indication of the inner polarity. In most people, each nostril is active for about 90 minutes. Throughout the day, the nostrils are changing and these changes are also deeply connected with the mental states. When the right nostril is active, one may react in an extroverted, expressive way. When the left nostril which is connected to the feminine side is open, one may respond in a more tolerant or introverted way. During the period of the change over, both nostrils may be active for a few minutes. In this period one may feel very light, very open and very accepting. In the case of a *Yogi*, both the nostrils are active all the time. This indicates the state that lies beyond duality.

The process of sublimation in *Hatha Yoga* can be illustrated by the example of milk. Milk in its natural state can stay fresh for 2 or 3 days. When this milk has been turned into curd or yoghurt, it may stay fresh for about a week. In India, butter is extracted from curd and butter may stay fresh for a month or so. Out of this butter, *Ghee* (clarified butter) is extracted and *Ghee* has unlimited shelf life and does not even require refrigeration. In India, *Ghee* is used in cooking and also in the *Yagnas* (fire sacrifices). When a little bit of *Ghee* is poured into the sacrificial fire, the fire gets rejuvenated. Milk represents the same *Prana* in the lower *Chakras* and *Ghee* represents the same *Prana* in the higher *Chakras*.

In one's day-to-day life, one hears people say that they are feeling low or they are feeling high. With the practice of *Yoga,* one understands this very clearly. Feeling high simply means that the *Prana* has moved up and the higher centres have opened leading to a feeling of expansion. Feeling low means that the energy has crashed, there is too much energy in the lower *Chakras* and not enough in the higher ones, which leads to a feeling of contraction.

This is also the meaning of *Brahmacharya. Brahmacharya* is usually translated as celibacy. Actually, it is composed of two words, *'Brahman'* meaning the highest Truth and *'Acharan'* meaning the way of life. So *Brahmacharya* means a way of life in which the Consciousness is directed towards the highest. From this perspective, even people who are married and have the Highest as their goal, can be called *'Brahmacharis'*.

This is the Indian way of looking at alchemy. In alchemy a base metal like lead is transformed into gold. The legend is that there is a philosophers stone, which when it touches the base metal, transforms it. When we practise *Yoga*, we understand that alchemy is actually the inner process of sublimation.

Classical *Yoga* is practised with breath, attention and minimum effort. In fact reducing the effort, in the *Asana*, is the practice. In one of the scriptures it is said that the *Asana* becomes perfect when the effort is zero. This is a unique situation because obviously one is making effort in the posture and yet there can be a feeling that no effort is being made. It is compared to the edge of a sword, where effort and effortlessness seem to blend into each other and one does not know any more what is what. Staying in this space for longer periods, allows deep-rooted unconscious patterns to emerge.

In the *Asana* practice, the very act of breathing sends the life force into the afflicted parts of the body. The life force follows the attention. This is the beauty of the practice, just holding the posture with attention in the body, allows healing to happen. The theory is that whatever is in the mind is also in the body. By removing the blocked energy in the body, one automatically starts to work on the blockages in the mind. That is why some people experience very intense mental purification in the early days of the *Yoga* practice. Initially they are surprised, because they thought they were working with the body and the results are being felt in the mind.

When one begins a *Yoga* practice, the most profound effect that one is usually not even aware of, is the state of freedom. With attention in the body and with breath awareness, one simply observes what comes up without trying to make the posture better. In this steady holding of the posture, periods of pure Awareness free of reactions, start to happen. The non-stop flow of thoughts, when experienced without craving and aversion, allows space to open. The mind is temporarily released from the stranglehold of cravings. In this state free of desire, one experiences oneself as Silence.

Even when *Yoga* is practised without any deep philosophical understanding, some of the hindrances start to be removed and spontaneous experiences of Silence manifest. Many people are surprised, even after a first *Yoga* class, to find that the relentless dialogue in the head has shut off. They may have a feeling of euphoria or exuberance. Some people experience a sense of expanded Awareness and there may be a feeling that the world is not closing in on them. These are all glimpses or attributes of the underlying Universal Silence that is present as everybody's Core.

Along with that, a large amount of energy that was locked up in these patterns of liking and disliking, gets freed up. In reality one is only experiencing a normal state of mind, free of duality. Because one constantly lives in a state of inner tension, the normal may feel extraordinary.

The advantage of the *Yoga* practice is that even if one does not understand all this and simply practises the *Yoga Asanas,* in a proper sequence, the effect will still be there. This is probably one of the main reasons for the popularity of *Yoga* today. It does not demand one to embrace a philosophy or subscribe to certain beliefs and yet the benefits are immediately very evident.

The state of *Yoga* is the state of *Chup Sadhana.* This distinction between *Yoga* as a practice and *Yoga* as a state, is important. *Yoga* as a practice is whatever we do as a practice and there are hundreds of different possibilities to choose from. The state of *Yoga* is the same, no matter what one's practice is. At this point, the practice becomes no practice,or just resting in Silence or abiding as Self.

SHAVASANA

The most important and least understood of the entire range of postures is the final relaxation called *Shavasana*. *Shavasana* means the corpse position. Many people are turned off by the word corpse and ask why it is not called a posture of relaxation and contentment. Why the insistence on such a morbid word.

At the end of the *Yoga* practice, *Shavasana* is practised for about ten minutes. Lying on the floor with legs and arms apart, one can ask the question, 'what effort am I making at the physical level to maintain this posture?' One will see that the breath is moving by itself, the gravity is pulling the body down by itself, different sensations and feelings are happening in the body all by themselves, the heart is beating by itself. In fact, there is absolutely nothing at the physical level that one can take credit for doing. It will become clear that one is doing absolutely nothing.

The next question is, 'what am I doing at the mental level?' Again one will find that thoughts are happening by themselves, feelings are happening by themselves, and memories are appearing and disappearing like bubbles, by themselves. It will be clear, that in all these mental activities there is no effort, no 'doing'.

Now, the third question is the most important, 'what am I doing when I am doing nothing?' The answer to this question, if the *Shavasana* is indeed *Shavasana*, is, 'I am doing nothing, I am the Awareness that is knowing these physical and mental activities'. The state of non-doing is also how the condition of death is described. However in *Shavasana* one is totally wide-awake and present. Only the illusion of 'doership' is not there. In this state of non-doing, only witnessing remains. This is the transcendent state of Presence in which all actions are seen as happening by themselves. According to Indian philosophy, ones true Self is this witnessing Consciousness. This is why this posture is not called a posture of relaxation because relaxation is something that is done. *Shavasana,* on the other hand is that which transcends doing and not doing.

The state of *Chup Sadhana*, a true *Shavasana* and Enlightenment are different names for the same reality.

यतो यतो निश्चरति मनश्चञ्चलमस्थिरम्।
ततस्ततो नियम्यैतदात्मन्येव वशं नयेत्॥

Yato-yato niścarati manaś cañcalam asthiram
Tatas-tato niyam y' aitad ātman y eva vaśaṁ nayet

Bhagavad Gita ch 6 verse 26

Mind is nothing but Awareness going outwards. It is easily impressed by the pleasant and unpleasant experiences and gets lost in them. This habit of constantly wandering away makes the mind restless, unsteady and weak.

Becoming aware of this tendency of the mind to wander out through the sense organs, becomes the practice. Of all the sense organs, the eyes and the ears are the major highways and living in fantasies and imagination is an even bigger highway. When the mind stops going out, it rests as Awareness in the heart and only meditation remains.

MEDITATION, DHYANA, SAMADHI

The word meditation has become very common and mainstream. Hardly anybody raises an eyebrow when somebody mentions that they meditate. Even doctors in hospitals and therapists recommend meditation as a means of accelerating recovery from illness.

In studies and translations of Indian scriptures, one sees that the *Sanskrit* word *'Dhyana'* is usually translated as meditation. *Dhyana*, however means attention and Awareness. For example if a child is crossing a busy road in Delhi, the mother will tell the child to cross with *'Dhyana'*. She is not asking the child to mediate while crossing the road. She is telling it to be aware, to be present.

When meditation is being discussed, there can be so many varieties of meditation and one can spend a whole day comparing and analysing them, but if Awareness or Presence is being discussed, there is not much to say. Presence in one person and the Presence in another are fundamentally the same.

Mostly, what is called meditation in the world, is actually *Dharana* which means concentration. Awareness when directed to a specific point, a mantra, the breath, an image, a sound etc. is not meditation but concentration. Concentration is also a very important step. When one's attention is fragmented and going in a hundred different directions, true meditation is very far away. Concentration practices help to gather this attention so that the next step of Awareness of Awareness can happen.

In the way the word meditation is usually used, it implies an action. We will go for a walk, we will have a cup of tea and then we will meditate. The flaw in all meditation practices is that they create a 'doer', a 'meditator'. This 'doer' is the ego self and the purpose of the practice is the dissolving of this ego self. That is why in India it is said that all practices create ego. Awareness or Self is, philosophically speaking, actionless. Simple Awareness is effortless. Awareness is the witnessing Self. This is the state of meditation. One cannot 'do' meditation, one can only 'be' Meditation. Meditation here has the same meaning as Awareness, as *Chup Sadhana*.

In many spiritual traditions, it is said that the mind is a big obstacle and there is talk of subduing or controlling the mind. This kind of thinking creates more duality because now, the mind thinks it has to kill the mind. In this way, the primary Consciousness gets split and becomes fragmented. A better way is to see that the mind is nothing but Awareness in action. Awareness externalized, going outwards as perceptions thoughts and feelings, becomes the mind.

Mānasam tu kim margane krite
Naiva mānasam mārga arjavāt
Upadesha Saram *Ramana Maharishi*
On seriously seeking, questioning and looking for
the mind, no such thing as a mind is found.
This is the direct path for dealing with the mind.

In the state of Silence, no mind is found.

One can compare this process to a tug of war in which the silent team is pulling the attention inwards and the noisy team is pulling the attention outwards. Sometimes, the silent team is stronger and abidance in Self happens easily. At other times, the noisy team is very strong and even with a lot of effort, abidance does not happen.

93

So instead of trying to kill the mind, bringing the attention to the heart and resting as Silence, becomes the path of *Chup Sadhana*.

Niḥsaṅgo niśkryo 'si twaṁ svaprakāśo nirañjanaḥ
Ayam eva hi te bandhaḥ samādhim anutiṣthasi

Ashtavakra Gita ch 1 verse 15

You are pure Awareness that has no contact with anything,
you are pure Awareness that is actionless,
you exist in your own light,
you are the proof of your own existence,
and there are no defects in you.
Your only bondage is, that you are trying to practise meditation,
when you are meditation.

The Sage Ashtavakra points this out to King Janaka.

In the third chapter of the *Yoga Sutras of Patanjali, Samadhi* is described as the state in which only the object of attention remains and the one observing, becomes empty. In other words the subject/object relationship dissolves.

There is only one state in which the subject, object and the verb become one. When the subject is Awareness, the object is Awareness and the process is Awareness. Only Awareness remains. This is the understanding of the Trinity. In every other experience the subject is different, the object is different and the verb is different.

The State of *Samadhi* is the State of Self or Silence aware of Itself. This State of Awareness or Presence is not an action. It is that existential State, which exists prior to actions and continues to exist after the actions are over. As soon as one gives it a name, distortion happens. Even to call it Silence, is already a distortion because Silence is seen to be the opposite of noise. That is why for the sake of clarity, one says, that Silence which is beyond silence and noise.

The missing link in all this is that 'I' cannot meditate because 'I am', already is Meditation. When I become quiet from inside and outside, in this thoughtless state, wanting nothing, having nothing and knowing nothing, what remains is Meditation.

अपाने जुह्वति प्राणं प्राणेऽपानं तथापरे ।
प्राणापानगती रुद्ध्वा प्राणायामपरायणाः ॥

Apāne juhvati prāṇaṁ prāṇe'pānaṁ tathā'pare
Prān'āpāna-gatī rudhvā prāṇāyāma-parāyaṇaḥ

Bhagavad Gita ch 4 verse 29

*Those who have understood that each breath arises from the
silent Source, have really understood the meaning of Pranayama.
For such people, the in-breath is born of Silence, the out-breath
merges into Silence and in the gap between the in-breath and
out-breath, Silence remains as the state of rest.*

BREATH & PURIFICATION

Observing the flow of the breath, the simple natural every-day breath moving through the nostrils, is a complete practice in itself. Watching the breath entering the nostrils and watching the breath leaving the nostrils. Without trying to improve the breath, without trying to make it longer. Just natural breath, as it is.

Watching the breath develops present moment Awareness and sharpens the instrument of attention. Watching the breath also creates purification of the mind. It can make the mind of the seeker free of obsessive patterns and distortions, thereby allowing 'That' which is behind the mental curtain to become visible. The breath, as an object of attention, is readily available to everybody 21,000 times a day. It is universal, real, non-conceptual and always in the present moment.

In fact, one can be confident that just this simple practice, followed for some time, can take one quite far on the inner journey. Also because one is working with real breath, with reality, the dangers of getting lost on the path are reduced. Simple breath-awareness will produce good results, even if one is following other practices or no practices.

This practice is not a breathing exercise, *Pranayama* or breath control. It is an exercise in Awareness. The effort is not to control the breath. One is simply conscious of the in-breath and out-breath for as long as possible, without allowing the attention to get distracted.

As soon as one starts, one finds out how difficult this is. One discovers that the mind does not want to be in the present moment, even for 5 seconds. One may barely watch three breaths and the mind will run away.

As one continues to watch, one will see that the mind runs either to the past or to the future. Living in the past and future is obviously ignorance. Truth, by its very definition is 'here and now'. What is needed is to develop the 'instrument' to be aware of the present moment. The simple watching of the breath develops the instrument.

The breath is always 'here and now' and is an actual physical experience. The breath touching the walls of the nostrils is not a concept. The touch is real and one can actually feel it. One also realizes that no two breaths are exactly the same. There is always some difference. This Awareness of the difference, is sensitivity. The main thing is to watch the breath as it is, without adding a word, a mantra, a concept to it. Just naked, raw breath. Even using the word 'breath' creates a slight distortion because the word 'breath' is not breath.

As the sensitivity grows, it becomes very clear that breath is intimately related to the mind. As the breath, so the mind. When one is angry, the breath becomes slightly hard. When one is depressed, there is a feeling of not getting enough air and one may sigh to relieve this constriction. When somebody is in a hostile environment, they may actually feel as if the air is poisoned.

By becoming aware of the breath, one also becomes aware of what is sitting in the deeper levels of the mind. As the breath becomes more subtle, more refined, the subtler levels of the mind start to get exposed. This can be quite a discovery. As the subtler layers are exposed, the memories, patterns and distortions present in them, also become apparent. This painful mental content will manifest as painful, uncomfortable feelings in the body. It may feel like raw nerve endings, like exposed wounds. The habitual pattern is to run away from the discomfort, to escape or somehow abort the process. However, if one understands what is happening, this becomes a great opportunity for purification and release from that, which one is carrying as baggage.

The simple theory is that pain and trauma get stuck in us due to lack of Awareness. The awareness contracts when confronted by pain. This contraction is the resistance. It does not allow the experience to pass through and paradoxically the more we don't like it, the more it haunts us.

The practice now is to do the opposite. If the disease is lack of Awareness and contraction, then the answer is more Awareness and expansion. As the memories, pain and patterns emerge from the subtler levels of the mind, one simply stays present with attention on the in-breath and the out-breath. Neither indulging nor resisting.

The breath is like a bridge between the conscious and unconscious mind. The breath is also the bridge between the physical body and the mind. As long as one stays in the bridge, one is safe from the powerful curent of the river. When one falls off the bridge, one is swept away by the turbulent mind. The surface, conscious mind knows what is right, what is wrong and what needs to be done. The problem is that the deep, unconscious mind does not care for the wisdom of the conscious mind. The unconscious mind reacts blindly like a wild animal that refuses to be controlled. One is continuously defeated by these unconscious patterns.

The Awareness of the breath removes the wall between the conscious and unconscious mind. This inner battle, where one part of the mind is trying to control the other part of the mind, comes to an end. The split mind becomes whole. One can say that the entire mind then becomes conscious. This is the place where one feels that the mind has no limits. In this state everything becomes possible because here whatever the mind imagines, it can also actualize.

Another way to look at the breath is through the metaphor of *Nama Rupa*. *'Nama, Rupa'* means mind/body. In the practice of *Yoga*, these are called *Citta* and *Prana*. It is said that these two emerge from a single Source. This Source is the foundation, the Silence. It is beyond duality, beyond time and beyond cause and effect. The Source is the uncreated Self, manifesting in an individual as the personal self.

Now if one wants to reach the Source of the mind/body, one could either use the breath or the thoughts. Watching the simple breath, with unbroken attention. Letting the breath become subtler and subtler. A point comes when one can experience the gap between the in-breath and out-breath. Then there is the birth of the subtlest breath. This subtlest breath emerges from Silence.

Similarly watching the thoughts without reacting, allows the thoughts to slow down. As the thoughts reduce, one will come to a point where the gap between two thoughts is experienced. The birth of a thought emerging from the Silence becomes clear. Abiding in the gap, even for short periods, is a great victory.

When the one silent Source behind the two is seen, the individual disappears. The individual is only a product of the duality. In the Source, there is no duality and therefore no individuals. Source is one and individuals are many. They cannot both appear at the same time. The appearance of the individual is the apparent disappearance of the Source and the appearance of the Source is the disappearance of the individual. That is why all religions talk of dissolving ego because the dissolving of the ego is the appearance of the Source. The missing link is that trying to dissolve the ego can create an even fatter ego.

In the Source, there is neither sin nor merit, neither defects nor perfection, neither spiritual nor non-spiritual, neither bondage nor liberation, neither affirmation nor denial. All these qualities are super-imposed on 'That' which is pristine and quality-less. The uniqueness of Indian philosophy is that instead of trying to remove the defects, disease and death, the attention is taken to the individual who is assumed to have the defects. When the Source is discovered, no individual is found. The defects and imperfections cannot exist by themselves. They need a 'somebody' to belong to. They cannot belong to 'nobody'. This is the most sublime purification practice.

Chup Sadhana is the practice of resting as Silence. When one is resting as Silence, one transcends all possible practices and connects with the Source that lies beyond all practices. All the possible practices are done in the field of *Nama Rupa*, body and mind. The fulfilment of all practices lies beyond *Nama Rupa*.

ब्रह्मार्पणं ब्रह्म हविर्ब्रह्माग्नौ ब्रह्मणा हुतम्।
ब्रह्मैव तेन गन्तव्यं ब्रह्मकर्मसमाधिना ॥

*Brahm'ārpaṇaṁ brahma havir brahm'āgnau brahmaṇā hutam
Brahm'āiva tena gantavyaṁ brahma-karma-sāmadhinā*

Bhagavad Gita ch 4 verse 24

When the underlying Source, Brahman is seen as the offering, as the act of offering, as the person making the offering and as the fire in which the offering is consumed, every action in life becomes a sacrifice leading to wisdom. The illusion of personal doership comes to an end when the one Source is seen as playing all the roles.

In that state of resting as Silence, resting as Brahman, the three Yogas of Karma, Bhakti and Jnana find their fulfilment.

KARMA, BHAKTI, JNANA YOGA

The eighteen chapters of the *Bhagavad Gita* can roughly be divided into three categories. The first six relate to the path of *Karma*, the next six to the path of *Bhakti* and the last six to the path of *Jnana*. Each of the chapters of the *Bhagavad Gita* is also called a *'Yoga'*.

In fact these are not really three separate paths. When understanding has dawned in a person because wisdom and devotion are both found in the heart, devotion is the result. At this point one cannot differentiate between wisdom and love. This devotion then expresses itself in day-to-day life through the actions of such a person. Such actions, in which the motivation is to sense others, are consecrated actions. This is *Karma Yoga*.

The three paths, address the different natures of the practitioners. Some people are very cerebral and enjoy reasoning and logic. For them study of the scripture and deciphering truths, may feel very exhilarating.

There are people in whom emotions are very strong and for them the path of love and devotion may be more relevant. They may find scriptures, arguments and reasoning very tedious. Then there are those who have neither the inclination for devotional practice nor possess discriminating intellect to study, for them the path of consecrated action, *Karma Yoga* is said to be the best.

KARMA YOGA

Karma in *Sanskrit* has two meanings, action and reaction. This is a way of saying that actions cannot be separated from reactions. Throughout one's life, from morning to night, one is performing actions both consciously and unconsciously. In the Indian way of looking, each of these actions brings a reaction and these reactions become patterns and tendencies that bind the Consciousness. Consciousness gets formatted by these patterns and tendencies and looses its inherent freedom and purity. The reactions of *Karma* are said to be like handcuffs. There is no escape. The purpose of the practice is to dissolve these shackles. These tendencies, patterns or *Karmas* follow the individualized consciousness from life to life, until at some point the *Karma* is eventually dissolved.

So one can say, the practice of *Karma Yoga* is to act in such a way that reactions do not bind and old programmed reactions get dissolved. New knots are not tied and old ones are unloosened.

In the *Bhagavad Gita*, the practice of *Karma Yoga* is described in several verses. One sees that what creates the bondage of *Karma* is not the action, rather the attachment to the fruit of the action. People act with a desire to gain happiness or to become free of pain. When a desire is fulfilled, one tends to get attached to the result and wanting that result again and again makes one greedy. This creates bondage. When the desire is not fulfilled, there is anger and frustration and that creates another kind of bondage.

The simple practice of *Karma Yoga* is to surrender the fruit of the action to God, in advance. The result of the action is not in one's hand and both wanted and unwanted fruits will create bondage. By surrendering the fruit of the action to God, one gets relieved of the anxiety about the outcome of the action and becomes free to act in the world fearlessly. If surrendering the fruit of the action to God does not speak to ones heart, one can surrender it to one's own highest ideal. For example, one can dedicate the fruit of the action to one's country, to one's family, to a cause.

The point is, to get out of this habit of constantly reacting and tying new knots. This becomes consecrated action because now whatever fruit comes, good or bad, does not belong to anybody. It leaves one unburdened.

Chup Sadhana can be summed up as a practice in which one is not reacting. Not reacting means watching and being present. In fact, reacting and not reacting are the only two choices in life. When one is able to be in a quiet state of acceptance, a new karmic knot is not tied and the old knots that come up because of not reacting, become loosened. When one reacts, a new knot is tied and this new knot becomes part of the old accumulated knots. The patterns get strengthened. In the practice of *Karma Yoga*, dedicating the action to God and offering the fruits of that action to God, one no longer has to react to the outcome. This state of being present in life without reacting and also without escaping, becomes purification.

There is another way of practising *Karma Yoga* which is more relevant to the *Yoga Asana* practice. In this method, one stays present in the here and now, remaining aware. The present moment is a thoughtless state, in which there is no ego. Ego or personal self is only a product of time, of past and future. In the present moment, there is nobody there. This 'nobody' is the expanded Awareness.

This form of *Karma Yoga* is the most sublime because here the very ego is offered into this expansion. Here staying present becomes surrender. In this state, one moves beyond the duality of consecrated and unconsecrated actions. The limited personal awareness expands into the Impersonal Universal Awareness. When this total Awareness acts, there is just action and the trinity of the actor, the action and the purpose of action are experienced as one movement. In simple language this can be called spontaneous action. Spontaneous actions have a different flavour, different fragrance and do not leave any binding residue.

Karma Yoga is a straightforward path. Actions are unavoidable in life and create bondage. The same actions, through a slight shift, become the means of liberation.

BHAKTI YOGA

A great saint, *Neem Karoli Baba*, who lived in the *Himalayas*, once summed up the entire devotional practice in one sentence 'love everyone, serve everyone and remember God'.

Bhakti means to serve, devotion, love etc. We can also look at *Bhakti* as a willingness to create space for a person or a situation, especially when it is difficult. Many people have the idea that we must love our enemies or we must not dislike the situation and if we dislike the situation, that is not *Bhakti*. In reality just the willingness to make space for a situation, even if we don't like it, is enough. The opposite of *Bhakti* would be to close the space and become contracted and dense.

When we look at devotion in this way, we see that this willingness to stay open and present in a difficult situation creates expansion in us and our vibration level rises. So we are not doing a favour to the person for whom we are creating space, rather it is a favour to ourselves. Expansion and contraction are really the two metaphors which describe the path of devotion.

Love and devotion are actually not actions, but states of Consciousness. Love is the quality of one's true Self that lives in the heart. In other words, one cannot 'do' love, one 'is' love. The individualized consciousness is a bundle of contradictions and is the enemy of love. Love does not happen between egos. In the state of love, the ego-self drops. The heart in one recognizes the heart in the other.

In many religions there is the idea to love God in order to find Truth. In reality, because love is the quality of one's Truth, finding love and finding Truth are one and the same.

Whether the love is for one's family or country or anything else, the love comes from the same place and whoever loves, gets elevated and expanded. That is why it is better to have loved and lost, than to have never loved at all. In love, even the losers become winners.

In India, many forms of God are worshipped. Some people make the mistake of thinking of these many forms as polytheism. In fact, it has always been understood that the forms are not important, it is the *Bhakti* that is generated towards these forms that is important.

Bhakti Yoga is said to be the safest of all paths because there is little danger of falling. In many practices, when success is achieved, there is a danger of pride and ego arising. This pride in the spiritual accomplishments maybe so subtle that one is not even aware of it. Pride is the reason behind the downfall in any practice. In the path of *Bhakti,* the worshipper has already made himself insignificant and the object of worship, has become everything. The worshipper considers himself to be already fallen so there is not so much danger of falling any further.

Bhakti with understanding means, the object of devotion is seen as an external symbol of one's true Self. An external form is created to awaken the *Bhakti* in the heart because hardly anybody is ready to accept the highest Truth as one's own Self.

The *Upanishads* emphatically declare that the highest Lord of the Universe lives in the body as one's own Self. In that case, everybody should be worshipping their own Self. There is a strong conviction that I am bad or useless or degraded, so these words of the scriptures do not have much impact. In this way, it becomes easier to satisfy the need to worship by creating an external form towards which the love can be directed. The individual in the head, surrenders to the Awareness in the heart by prostrating in front of an external symbol.

Bhakti is also said to be the path of the 'higher taste'. In the state of devotion, in the love of God, one experiences very sublime, super-sensual states. When these higher states happen, everything else pales in comparison and coming out of bondage becomes effortless.

The state of *Bhakti* and the experience of *Chup Sadhana* are the same. When bliss of devotion is felt in the heart, the jumping of the mind comes to an end and one is quite happy to rest as the silent Presence.

JNANA YOGA

Traditionally, *Jnana* means wisdom, knowledge, practices, scriptures, insights etc. The obstacle in talking about *Jnana Yoga* or the path of knowledge is that *Jnana* gets treated like a commodity. In books, in spiritual literature or advertisements for retreats, *Jnana* or knowledge is treated as a product to be gained.

Jnana does not only mean knowledge, it also means the 'Knowing Principle'. That Consciousness in which knowledge is gained. *Jnana*, in that sense, is a synonym for Awareness, Self and Being.

The highest knowledge is the knowledge of the Knower. When one talks of gaining knowledge, a duality of the Knower and the known gets created. In the practice of *Chup Sadhana* one rests as Silence. Awareness instead of streaming out, stays at home. This is the meaning of knowing the Knower.

Jnana Yoga can also be said to be the understanding which is obtained from studying scriptures. Scriptures are like a map that shows the location of the hidden treasure. Scriptures contain hidden clues, little hints that point to the truth in one's heart.

As is seen in the world, scriptures themselves over time start to get worshipped instead of what they were pointing to. People talk of the holy Bible, the sacred *Gita*, the holy *Koran* etc. with such conviction and start treating the books as sacred, instead of understanding that what is being pointed to, is holy and sacred.

The content of Consciousness, no matter how sublime, is not wisdom. It is the context, which is knowing the contents, that is sacred. The context is another name for Awareness. This Awareness is Silence. Therefore it is said that the highest knowledge is transmitted in Silence. The missing link is, that the knowledge is not transmitted in Silence, rather the Silence is the transmission in which the individual seeker disappears.

त्रिविधं नरकस्येदं द्वारं नाशनमात्मनः ।
कामः क्रोधस्तथा लोभस्तस्मादेतत्त्रयं त्यजेत् ॥

Tri-vidhaṁ narakasy'edaṁ dvāraṁ nāśanam ātmanaḥ
Kāmaḥ krodhas-tathā lobhas tasmād etat trayaṁ tyajet

Bhagavad Gita ch 16 verse 21

The delusion, that happiness exists outside one's Self, makes one greedy. Greed creates desire, and when a desire is not fulfilled, there is anger. The three together; greed, desire and anger, build very strong patterns that create bondage.

Self, which in its natural state is unbounded, starts to feel trapped and contracted. This contracted place is hell, and greed, desire, and anger are the three doors to hell. So avoiding these three doors is a good idea.

CONTRACTION & EXPANSION

Chup Sadhana can also be seen using the metaphor of contraction and expansion. In the practice of physical *Yoga*, this can be understood in the context of the *Chakras*.

The *Chakras* represent the junction points through which consciousness manifests. In the lower *Chakras*, consciousness vibrates at a lower or slower frequency. In the higher *Chakras*, consciousness vibrates at a higher frequency. The lower the vibrations, the more dense and resisting the consciousness. The higher the vibrations, the more permissive and open the consciousness.

In a completely expanded state of total Awareness, there is absolutely no resistance. This is one end of the spectrum. The other end could be called a state of complete contraction, in which there is darkness, density, pain and finally insanity. The experiences of life happen between these two extremes.

When one resists anything, this resistance is a contraction in one's own consciousness. When one accepts, one is willing to create space in oneself. If this principle is understood, one has a complete practice. Every event in life, pleasant or unpleasant, can become a means for expansion. This is the essence of *Bhakti*, the devotional path. In the devotional path, one feels that God is omnipresent. That whatever comes up in life is only an aspect of God or happens by God's will. So the event, especially when it is unpleasant, is not just tolerated, but accepted as a sacrament. This is how one learns to love one's enemies. Love here does not mean to generate an emotion, but just to create the space in one's own Awareness, to allow that event to be and not try to squeeze it out.

When one does not want to create space for an event, one will use judgement, logic and fear to block it out. When one lives unconsciously, it appears that one is hurting someone by excluding them. When consciousness expands, one sees that one was only hurting oneself, by creating a contraction in oneself.

When we read in the religious books, 'love your neighbour', 'love God', 'have love for the poor and suffering', it is all meant to expand and when expansion has happened, to expand further.

Contraction, is the condition of the individual self in identification. Expansion is the natural state of the Self in the heart. So actually there are no strategies to expand and contract. Understanding the principle is important. The major religions in the world, address contraction and expansion using the metaphor of good and evil, God and Satan, heaven and hell etc. From the religious perspective, certain actions take us far away from God and certain actions bring us closer to God. If one looks at the Ten Commandments in the Bible, one will see them as techniques for avoiding contraction. In other places one will see methods of creating expansion.

The individual is nothing but a series of contractions. The head is full of desires, fears, anxieties, tensions, worries and hopes. The narrower the consciousness the more the conflicts. In dense, contracted states, the vibration frequency tends to be low. Everything in creation, without exception, has certain vibration levels. When one walks around feeling low, which means that the vibration level is low, the world will be seen to be vibrating too fast. To such a person, the world will appear out of control and overwhelming. To resolve this feeling of being out of control, one tries to exercise more control. This is the origin of the power trip. The more dense and withdrawn the awareness, the more one will try to assert control and the more out of control one will feel. There will be a feeling of wanting to control disorderly people, the need to move out of the country or in some way to try and escape.

When the Awareness is expanded, the vibrations are much higher, and in contrast the world will appear to move in slow motion. The world will be seen like a playground in which children are playing. It will feel totally non-threatening. The higher the vibrations, the more beautiful the world will look. It will seem that there is enough time for everything. That feeling of being out of control will not be there. That expanded Awareness has enough room to accommodate the many complexities and contradictions of life.

When people relate to each other, it is seldom that both are expanded or contracted to the same degree. In every relationship there is a natural process of seeking a point of stability, where the levels of expansion are about equal. In many relationships, when one person starts a practice and the other doesn't, a gulf can appear in the vibration level. The law of nature is such, that it will seek to stabilize the levels. This means that either the one vibrating at a higher frequency will lift the one vibrating at a lower frequency but more likely the one vibrating at a lower frequency, will bring down the one vibrating at a higher frequency. Either the stability will come, or the vibration levels will move so far apart that there will be a complete disintegration in that relationship.

This explains why so many people feel that going home after a retreat can be a deflating experience. People at home will not seem supportive. The important thing is to realize that it is not personal and nobody is deliberately trying to bring the other person down. It is just laws of nature operating. Similarly, when one starts a practice one may find in time, certain old friendships or old relationships, naturally falling away. In one's diet, place of work and interests, changes start to appear spontaneously.

In the world, everybody is like a tuning fork, an emitter of vibrations. This means that at whatever level one is vibrating, people in that person's surroundings pick up those vibrations and are affected by them. In the same way people's vibrations, both individually and collectively, are being picked up by each one of us. When we go and sit for a few minutes with a person whose vibration levels are high, we also start to get lifted and begin to feel like millionaires.

When we spend time in an environment where the vibration levels are low, after some time, we may start to feel very low and depleted. Living in a world full of anxious, fearful, greedy people, it is almost impossible for an individual to maintain an expanded level of consciousness. There are only two ways to get by. Either one is part of a spiritual group, and benefits from a group energy of some kind, where the level of consciousness is high; or one has one's own individual practice. The kind of practice does not matter, as long as it suits one's temperament.

The simplest way to raise the vibration level is just to love and accept everything. This is a very effective *Mantra*. This love and acceptance is not passivity, rather a state of intense silent warmth. A feeling of deep inner relaxation. Love means, to love oneself even for not being able to love. Similarly acceptance does not mean to become a masochist and put up with everything, rather just to stay present with the experience and see what happens. Seeing whatever is arising inside and outside. For those who can do this, no other practice is necessary.

Sound exists at various frequencies. The highest frequency of sound is said to be Silence. This Silence is not a state of absence, rather a state of dynamic Presence. This Silence is the Self. Therefore, a state of complete acceptance, in which nothing is excluded, is Self-realization. This understanding is both the practice and the goal of *Chup Sadhana*.

अनन्याश्चिन्तयन्तो मां ये जनाः पर्युपासते ।
तेषां नित्याभियुक्तानां योगक्षेमं वहाम्यहम् ॥

Ananyāś cintayanto māṁ ye janāḥ paryupāsate
Teṣām nity'ābhiyuktānām yoga-kṣeman vahām y aham

Bhagavad Gita ch 9 verse 22

There are those who have understood that the Source of everything is always present in the heart as the Self. For such people staying in the heart, effortlessly, is the highest form of worship. Proximity becomes worship.

Self recognizing Self, is the play of love. In this state of surrender, the Source acts like a mother, nurturing, protecting and fulfilling all the needs.

PRAYER & SURRENDER

The limited personal self, imagining itself to be helpless, small, defenceless, a victim of circumstances, subject to disease, death, old age and a dozen other dilemmas, prays for the fulfilment of desires and for protection from calamities.

From the perspective of Indian philosophy, the Self present in the heart, is the Lord of the Universe, the Master of delusion and for whom all things are possible. As long as the conviction of being an individual self exists, one prays to an almighty God for the resolution of one's difficulties. Whether God is imagined to live in heaven, or is imagined as one's own Self, prayer is equally effective.

Simply put, prayer is a state of surrender. Being in the heart or coming out of the head, is surrender. The individual conditioned self, realizing it's powerlessness, bows down and is willing to step aside. This willingness of the false self or ego self to step down, is the opening of the door to the dungeon where the unconditioned Self has been kept imprisoned.

The true Self's arrival on the scene is the resolution of the problem. The true Self is already free and complete. The true Self does not answer the prayer but is the answer.

One can look at prayer in another way. Everything one could possibly want is already present as one's Self. The deep-rooted identification with the body makes one feel vulnerable and powerless. The needs of the body feel like one's own needs and the fears of the body become one's own fears. When one prays intensely, the prayer removes the barrier of the conditioning and reveals the heart where the prayer is already answered.

Another way to understand prayer, is that in a sense all desires are prayers and all prayers get answered sooner or later. The problem is that due to a state of unconscious living, many desires exist in contradiction to one another. For example one may have a desire to eat a lot of food and also a desire to be slim. So these two prayers would cancel each other out. One may desire to have a peaceful, uncomplicated life and also seek complex relationships.

As one becomes quieter and quieter through *Chup Sadhana* or whatever practice one is following, one finds that the thinning out of desires and the appearance of Silence are the same thing. Desires create a wall between individual awareness and the Universal Awareness. As the desires dissolve, this artificial separation also dissolves, and individuality and Universality become one silent space. In this Silence, in this state of 'nothing' all joy is seen as the joy of the Source. At this stage, desires which were so important, start to feel like disturbances, and the desire-less state is seen as the state of Grace.

The highest prayer would be to pray to God for that state, in which one never has to pray for anything again. In other words, when God is experienced as one's Self, then what is there left to pray for. The personal limited self, realizing that it was always the unlimited Universal Self, is the state of *Yoga*. Again, it is not that one self is joining the other Self, which is what the word *Yoga* as union implies, rather it is the realization that there never were two separate selves. Realization is not an achievement, it is just an understanding, just a shift in perspective.

In this way of looking, prayer and *Yoga* are the same thing. One could say that if it is absolutely not possible for somebody to practise *Yoga*, one can pray for Grace and reach the same state. Each prayer is an invocation, whether one is praying to this God or that God, or this statue or that statue, or this name or that name. All prayers go to the place of truth in one's own heart. All prayers are answered from the same place. Even a prayer for material success and for mundane things, becomes a means of knocking on that door.

Any sincere prayer brings the attention from the head into the heart. In fact, that is the complete spiritual journey.

सुखमात्यन्तिकं यत्तद्बुद्धिग्राह्यमतीन्द्रियम् ।
वेत्ति यत्र न चैवायं स्थितश्चलति तत्त्वतः ॥

Sukham ātyanikaṁ yat tad buddhi-grāhyam atīndriyam
Vetti yatra na c'aiv'āyaṁ sthitaś calati tattvataḥ

Bhagavad Gita ch 6 verse 21

The seeker encounters this uncreated, causeless Bliss, the intensity of which does not seem to have any boundaries. This happiness is not an object that can be grasped by the senses or the mind. It is experienced by the Self, as the Self, when one becomes quiet.

Having found this unlimited Source of peace and happiness, one feels a disinclination to go anywhere else. The fickle and unsteady nature of the mind comes to an end because what one was seeking has been found. In the same way an ant, on finding a heap of sugar, never feels like leaving it.

YOGA OF HAPPINESS

What a person on the path of *Yoga* is seeking and what a so-called worldly person is seeking, is really the same thing. One can call it happiness, love, fulfilment or as the *Buddha* called it 'release from suffering'.

In the Indian way of looking, Self is unconditioned bliss. Not happiness because happiness has an opposite and because happiness is dependant upon certain conditions happening, rather bliss or ecstasy which has no opposite. It is said that other than Self there is no happiness.

Any desire tends to restrict this unconditioned blissful state by creating time. One day my desire will be fulfilled and I will be happy, is the great delusion. The unconditioned state is always now. Over time the desire, that began with a single thought, by repeated recollection, becomes a big hard knot.

The paradox is, that in the desire for happiness, desire itself becomes the biggest block to ever finding happiness. This is a built in problem with every desire. Every desire is saying that the present moment is not okay. This feeling of the present not being okay, creates a certain tension, a certain fever, a state of craving. This craving becomes a thorn which does not allow one to be present in the moment. Freedom is the state of 'here and now', and craving, which takes one out of the 'here and now' cannot co-exist. Craving keeps one from being in the Source.

This abidance in the Source, means to be fulfilled in the moment. Before a desire arises, there is desirelessness, after a desire is fulfilled, there is desirelessness. After making all the effort to fulfil the desire, one arrives back at the place where one started, the space of desirelessness. The question is, can one stay in this desireless place, is the Source, even when a desire has arisen in the mind.

This question of desires can be illustrated by a wall, made up of different sized round stones. Some stones are small, some stones are big. Behind the wall is the sun. When one of the stones is removed, a hole in the wall appears and the sunlight is experienced as warmth and radiance. In this example, the wall is the mind and the stones are the many desires, which constitute the mind. When one of the stones is removed, when one of the desires is fulfilled, the happiness or love that one feels, is the result of the sunlight steaming through the gap. This sunlight is the light of Self, which is not other than bliss. When a small desire is fulfilled, the light may not seem very bright, but when a big stone is removed, a big desire is satisfied, the light may feel very intense.

However, hardly has a desire been fulfilled, then the dialogue in the head starts to create a new desire,. Within a short period of time, that hole which had opened in the wall, gets filled up with a new stone, a new desire. That is why one finds that whatever it is in life, that once gave happiness, in time stops giving the same happiness.

When that which one was seeking is gained, temporarily the mind is free of craving. This open space allows the happiness behind the mind to shine. The happiness that one experiences in the fulfilment of a desire is not due to the fulfilment of the desire, rather is due, to the desireless state of mind that has been brought about. So paradoxically, the happiness is coming from a state of renunciation.

If we ask ten different people 'what do you get when you get what you want?' People may answer by saying that they will get happiness, peace of mind, removal of suffering or relaxation. On close examination one finds, that what one gets is a desireless state, and in this state one gets one's Self. One is able to rest as one's Self. To put it another way, one experiences an unfragmented state, a feeling of wholeness and completeness. This is happiness. One does not get happiness, one discovers oneself to have been happiness all along.

Due to an intense delusion in the world, happiness is always being attributed to the fulfilment of desire. One gets addicted to this habit of desiring. It becomes a pattern to live in a constant state of desiring something. This desiring becomes like a perpetual itch. One feels a need to scratch and the scratching temporarily feels good. When one stops scratching, there is a need to scratch again and like this the craving gets stronger. After some time, it feels completely natural to live in a state of constant craving. Real happiness, which is simply a state free of craving and aversion, moves far away. In India it is said, that to think one can achieve happiness by fulfilling desires, is to believe that one can put out a fire by pouring *Ghee* on it.

The *Yogi* seeks the truth about his existence. Even though the *Yogi* seeks Truth by turning away from the objects of desire, he finds the same happiness that worldly people find when they are happy. At a superficial level it seems that these two paths are completely different. Through practice they are found to bring one to the same place. The big difference is that the *Yogi* experiences first hand happiness, and people in world experience second hand happiness.

In second-hand happiness, one first projects the happiness that is already present in one's heart, outwards onto a person, an object, a place, a particular type of food. Upon gaining that object of desire one experiences happiness. The problem is that this happiness gained, creates bondage, because of the delusion, that the happiness has come from a particular person or object. The *Yogi,* on the other hand, experiences happiness as his own Self. In this there is no delusion and this experience becomes liberating. Liberating, because when this happiness is seen as not other than one's Self, how can one lose it. One can lose everything, but one cannot lose oneself. People say they lost their key, they lost their house, they lost their way but nobody will say that they lost themselves.

Whatever has been said about happiness, can also be said about love. In the world, love, happiness, truth, beauty are considered different things. When understanding happens, it is seen that all these wonderful qualities, are really different facets of one Reality. This Reality is one's Self. That is why it does not matter which quality is being used to describe the inner experience.

The bottom line is, that the seeker of happiness is happiness. The seeker of love is love.

Becoming quiet inside and outside, ending the relentless seeking for answers, for love, for meaning, for purpose and resting as the ever-present Silence is *Chup Sadhana*.

यत्तदग्रे विषमिव परिणामेऽमृतोपमम् ।
तत्सुखं सात्त्विकं प्रोक्तमात्मबुद्धिप्रसादजम् ॥

Yat tad agre viṣam iva pariṇame 'mṛt'opamam
Tat sukham sāttvikaṁ proktam ātma-buddhi-prasāda-jam

Bhagavad Gita ch 18 verse 37

In the early days of practice, Sattvic happiness (born of purity) does not seem like happiness at all. On the contrary, it may appear like poison, devoid of any excitement, a state of crushing boredom, where one has turned away from both pleasure and pain.

When one is willing to stay in this 'no man's land', this same experience, which seemed like poison, in time turns into nectar. This Bliss arises from one's own Self in the heart and is not dependant on anything outside.

BOREDOM AS AN OPPORTUNITY

Yogaś citta vṛitti nirodaḥ

Yoga Sutras of Patanjali ch 1 aphorism 2

Yoga is a state in which there are no movements of the mind.

This can also mean the gap between two thoughts. The space in which nothing is happening, nothing happened and nothing will ever happen; a state beyond time and causation. The Awareness that is present in this gap is the true Self. This Self-realization is liberation.

Interestingly, this empty space is also how most people will describe boredom. Boredom either becomes an opportunity for liberation or a trap that takes one into hell. Most people do not think of boredom as a great disease, even though it is actually the primary cause behind most diseases.

Essentially boredom is a state in which there is neither pleasure nor pain. A person who is in pain is hurting, but not bored. Boredom is a condition of the false self. The false self needs four conditions to exist: the condition of craving and aversion or liking and disliking, and the condition of time, past and future.

The state of boredom is a condition in which there is neither pleasure and pain, nor anything to look forward to in the future. In this state, the false self feels like it is falling apart. The false self may feel as if it is being deprived of vital nourishment. That is why boredom for many people may feel like a slow agonizing death. People would rather die than be bored. Wars are started out of boredom. Extramarital affairs happen out of boredom. People gossip out of boredom. People engage in dangerous sports out of boredom.

The place of boredom, in which the duality of pain and pleasure are absent, is also the point from where the spiritual journey begins. Pain and pleasure are conditions of the mind. Behind the mind is one's true Self, which is made up of ecstasy. Boredom becomes an opportunity to come into ecstasy, when there is a willingness to stay in that condition of boredom, and allow the accompanying loneliness to come up. It is like passing through a gap, through a narrow gate. This gap, this gate is not always visible. One has to be patient and watchful.

The false self can be compared to a clockwork toy, which is continuously being wound up. The different tensions that are generated, the many concerns, the fears, the likes and dislikes, are continuously winding up this toy. Adding a little more tension each day becomes like an addiction. So one can say, the false self is just a bundle of tensions, and increasing those tensions, makes the false self feel more substantial.

If one stops winding up the toy and just leaves it alone, the toy will start unwinding and not stop until it is completely unwound. This is the emptying of the content of consciousness. There is nothing to do, one just has to stay in the situation, and digest whatever comes up. Whatever comes up, will be whatever one has consumed in life. If one has eaten fish, the breath will smell of fish.

To want freedom, more than anything else that the world has to offer is what is needed. In the religious sense, it means to love God more than anything else. It is a rare individual, who wants freedom above all else.

When the content of consciousness has been fully digested, what is revealed is the state of aloneness. In one of scriptures, this is illustrated by the example of peeling an onion. Removing one layer of the onion, the next layer is revealed. When all the layers have been removed, one by one, in the end there is nothing left. This 'nothing' is aloneness. This is the simple practice of *Chup Sadhana*. This aloneness is also called *'Kaivalya'* in *Sanskrit*, which means the unconditioned state, the Source, independent of all circumstances.

Even though aloneness may seem similar to loneliness, it is it's exact opposite. This state of aloneness is Self at rest in the heart. It is a state of fullness. Loneliness on the other hand, is a condition of deprivation experienced by the false self.

As a practical experiment, one can put oneself in a very boring situation, with no escapes and no exit strategies. Then as the boredom increases, one asks oneself the question, 'who is bored?' As one stays with the question quietly, there may be a feeling that, the questioner is dissolving. What is left over is just a feeling of quietness, peacefulness and comfort.

Very few people are willing to walk the spiritual path because it leads through the doorway of boredom, and everyone wants to avoid boredom at all costs. The familiar as boredom is strangling us yet the thought of leaving the boredom behind and entering the unfamiliar can be even more terrifying.

For the ego self, the present moment is never complete. In any situation one is looking forward to something. When there is nothing to look forward to, one calls that boredom. There is a constant need to create the next moment and the next moment is a projection of the past, so the present moment never comes. That is why the present moment for most people becomes a moment of intense boredom but for those on the spiritual path it becomes a doorway to heaven.

For most people, boredom and loneliness go hand in hand. In fact, one may not be able to differentiate between them. When one is in company, the people around become reflecting mediums. We are all reflecting back each other's existence and that makes us feel that we exist. That is why in the prison systems, solitary confinement which could be a great blessing, is treated as the worst punishment.

The study of boredom is the most fascinating subject. If one looks for boredom, no boredom is found and one will never have to be bored again. The solution to boredom lies in boredom, whereas everybody is trying to find the solution to boredom outside.

Aloneness is Self, Self is God, and God is that which exists beyond boredom and non-boredom. Resting quietly in that aloneness in which all possible experiences are present as potentiality, is *Chup Sadhana.*

पितासि लोकस्य चराचरस्य
त्वमस्य पूज्यश्च गुरुर्गरीयान्।
न त्वत्समोऽस्त्यभ्यधिकः कुतोऽन्यो
लोकत्रयेऽप्यप्रतिमप्रभाव ॥

Pitā'si lokasya car'ācarasya
tvam asya pūjyaś ca gurur garīyān
Na tvat-samo'sty abhyadhikah kuto'nyo
loka-traye'py apratima prabhāva

Bhagavad Gita ch 11 verse 43

The Self is present in the heart, as the Source and origin of all beings, the father and mother of all phenomena, whether moving or unmoving.

This innermost Self abiding in the heart, is the original Guru that is worthy of being worshipped. This one teacher, manifests as all the teachers that one encounters in life. There is nothing in the universe that can be compared to the infinite possibilities and power of this Guru.

GURU, SELF & GOD

The syllable *'Gu'*, means darkness and the syllable *'Ru'* means light. The one who brings light into darkness is the *Guru*. In other words, the one who removes darkness is the *Guru*. Darkness is the state of ignorance in which awareness is identified with the form and does not know itself. Light, is that same Awareness becoming aware of Itself. So the *Guru* is not a person and not an individual. The expanded Awareness in the heart is the *Guru*.

When a seeker is not ready to consider the Awareness itself as the *Guru*, that Awareness needs to manifest externally as a person. That external manifestation, in a form, is what most people consider a *Guru*.

A *Guru*, who thinks he is a *Guru*, is not a *Guru*. Awareness identified with the form is ignorance. How can someone who is stuck in ignorance, remove the ignorance in another. The realization that the same Awareness is the Self, *Guru* and God, is wisdom. This understanding is the culmination of the *Guru*/disciple relationship.

The *Guru* is not a person, but rather is that which reveals the Self in the heart. One can say, that potentially, any event could be the *Guru*. Falling in love could be the *Guru*, an act of great kindness could be the *Guru*, an experience of great beauty could be the *Guru*, even a drug-induced experience could be the *Guru*.

All relationships in life exist in duality. There need be two or more for a relationship to exist. Relationships perpetuate and create new relationships. The relationship with the *Guru* is the only relationship, which even though starting in duality, brings one to a place where that duality and all other dualities come to an end. That Source in which all relationships return home. That state of relationship before any relationships happened.

In Indian scriptures, one reads in several places that without a *Guru*, one cannot reach liberation. These statements can sometimes create neurotic relationships. One person gets stuck in the role of a *Guru* and anther gets stuck in the role of a student. The ego selves in both, instead of dissolving, become more substantial.

As the level of consciousness rises, the understanding of what is meant in the scriptures becomes clear. The individual seeker is pure Awareness identified with a bundle of thoughts. These thoughts are the conditioning. One can say that the seeker is 'Nothing' plus conditioning. All the effort made by the conditioning can only produce more conditioning. Anything multiplied by zero can only produce zero. The path and the practices that a seeker chooses, are coloured by the conditioning.

The *Guru* is that Presence in which the conditioning has come to an end. In this space, a seeker may become willing, out of love and faith, to drop the bundle of his conditioning. In this unconditional surrender, the seeker puts aside everything, all that he knows. When the seeker puts aside all that is known, the beliefs, the patterns, the convictions and becomes empty, the liberated state remains. The Self in the heart, which was covered up by this enormous quantity of the 'known', becomes free. Freedom is freedom from the 'known'. The dropping of the bundle of beliefs and conditions, is the revelation that Self, *Guru* and God are the same.

It is not that one surrenders to a *Guru* and then the *Guru* gives some special knowledge to that person. The *Guru* does not need the surrender of the seeker. In the surrender, the seeker disappears and wisdom dawns. The identity of the 'surrenderer', in the form of the seeker, is discovered to have been a phantom all along. This is true surrender. The surrender in which the 'surrenderer' is not found. Silence remains as ones true identity.

Resting as Silence in the practice of *Chup Sadhana* is the highest surrender. Silence, present as one's Self, is the greatest *Guru*. The willingness to put aside whatever has happened, whatever is happening and whatever will happen, allows the ever-present Self to shine.

बन्धुरात्मात्मनस्तस्य येनात्मैवात्मना जितः ।
अनात्मनस्तु शत्रुत्वे वर्तेतात्मैव शत्रुवत् ॥

Bandhur ātmā'tmanas tasya yen'ātm'aiv'ātmanā jitaḥ
Anātmanas tu śatrutve vartet'ātm'aiva śatruvat

Bhagavad Gita ch 6 verse 6

❻

Self, present in the heart is Silence, peace and tranquillity. When it moves out in the world of form, identification with the forms happen and multiple selves arise. The Self loses it's unbounded, unlimited nature, and experiences itself as trapped in the various personalities. Having lost the ability to witness, it becomes a 'doer' of actions and gets bound up by the reactions. These multiple selves, born of action, become the enemies of peace and tranquillity.

CONFUSION OF EGO & FALSE SELF

When scriptures have been translated from *Sanskrit* into other languages, often the word *'Ahamkara'* is translated as 'ego'. In *Sanskrit, Ahamkara,* has a very clear, distinct meaning. *Ahamkara* is a combination of two words. *'Aham'*, meaning 'I', the silent, formless Awareness and *'akara'*, meaning, 'form'. Therefore, *Ahamkara* is the silent formless Self, mistakenly identified with the form. Out of this confusion of identities, an individual person limited in space and time appears.

An example will illustrate this predicament. There is a thread and there are flowers. The flowers are strung on the thread and a garland is born. Now a third entity, a garland, has been produced which did not exist before. This is the birth of the ego. The thread represents Awareness and the flowers represent the different conditions of the body and mind. The interesting thing is, that even though a third entity called the garland has been produced, in reality there are still only two things: the thread and the flowers. This is the important point, that even though the ego is appearing, there is no ego.

The Seer, who is nothing but pure witnessing energy, becomes identified with the energy of a thought, a feeling or a body condition. This identification leads to multiple personalities appearing and disappearing. The multiple personalities are all super-imposed on the conditionless Awareness. The point is, that no matter how disastrous the conditions, how terrible the life, the State of Awareness remains pristine and is never contaminated.

For example, 'I am', which is formless, in identification with a young body becomes 'I am young'. The same 'I am' gets identified with an endless range of qualities: 'I am' old, 'I am' beautiful, 'I am' Indian, 'I am' American, 'I am' wise, 'I am' stupid. In the same way the 'I am' in identification experiences itself in an endless range of relationships, 'I am' a woman, 'I am' a man, 'I am' a mother, 'I am' a daughter, 'I am' a boss, 'I am' a brother. The same identification process applies to the emotions: 'I am' becomes happy, 'I am' becomes sad etc.

The word 'ego' on the other hand has a completely different meaning. It means somebody who is very proud, who thinks a lot of himself, who is opinionated and who thinks he is better than others. Especially in the West, people may think that eradication of the ego means the eradication of these negative qualities.

From the Indian perspective, trying to eradicate the ego, is the most subtle act of the ego. The 'I am' now becomes the ego-eradicator. The great saint, *Ramana Maharishi* said that using the ego to find the ego, is like asking a policeman to catch a thief when the policeman is himself a thief in disguise.

Many people maybe aware of the constant, non-stop dialogue in the head. There may be a feeling of a shadowy, ghostly person in the head, who is always criticizing, taunting and doubting. There may also be a feeling that there are several people having a conversation. This dialogue in the head, is the false self.

On examination, one finds that all this chattering is made up of four kinds of thoughts: thoughts of craving, aversion, past and future. The false self cannot ever be 'here', because 'here' is a state free of craving and aversion. Just simple acceptance and presence. The false self can also never be 'now', because it is always seeking something which creates time and 'doership'.

The elimination of this false self is the goal of all religious practices. The joke is, that, that which is to be eliminated, does not exist in the first place. So to make the garland disappear, all one has to do is to separate the thread from the flowers. In the same way to make the false self disappear, all one has to do is to be present. Awareness free of liking and disliking, free of resisting. Awareness, then experiences Itself as complete and the body and mind become expressions of that Completeness.

This phantom self, because it is false and an impostor constantly engages in actions and reactions, to give itself some substance and credibility. Because it is hollow and empty, it seeks to fill itself with possessions and relationships. Because of its need to survive at any cost, various obsessive, compulsive behaviour patterns get formed. It fills itself with food, opinions, points of view, judgements etc. Because it does not exist, it constantly seeks to justify its existence by becoming important. It increases its importance by always taking credit for actions that are actually happening spontaneously. Because it takes credit for actions, it also has to bear the consequences of the actions: feeling guilt about the past and anxiety about the future.

This is perhaps what is meant by the example in the Bible, about it being easier for a camel to pass through the eye of a needle, than for a rich man to enter the kingdom of heaven. The rich man is not a person with a lot of money, rather it is the fattened false self with all its baggage. As Awareness develops and the false self dissolves, the 'nobody' that is left can easily pass through the eye of a needle.

Awareness and the objects of awareness have very distinct and separate natures. This recognition is wisdom. Awareness is never changing and that which one is aware of, is never still even for a second. Awareness is formless and without boundaries. The objects of awareness have forms, whether physical or mental, and always exist in boundaries. Awareness is timeless and all the objects of Awareness, no matter what, exist in space and time. Awareness is complete and fulfilled, whereas the conditions of life are always incomplete and have a trace of dissatisfaction. Awareness is Silence and the objects of awareness are noise.

In the practice of *Chup Sadhana*, as one gradually becomes quiet for short periods, the velocity and the quantity of thoughts get reduced little by little. It may not happen right away, but each time one becomes quiet, the quietness acts like a brake. The car may not stop immediately, but it will slow down. Then very naturally, the gaps between the thoughts become evident. *Chup Sadhana* is the practice of abiding in these silent spaces between thoughts. Nothing has to be done. There are no tricks. Just becoming quiet and seeing what happens without resisting.

भोक्तारं यज्ञतपसां सर्वलोकमहेश्वरम्।
सुहृदं सर्वभूतानां ज्ञात्वा मां शान्तिमृच्छति ॥

Bhoktāraṁ yajña-tapasāṁ sarva-loka-maheśvaram
Suhṛdam sarva-bhūtānāṁ jñātvā māṁ śantiṁ ṛcchati

Bhagavad Gita ch 5 verse 29

All the difficult practices, austerities and sacrifices performed by the individual in life, are to reveal the expanded Awareness, the Lord of the Universe, residing in the heart as one's innermost Self. The recognition that this Awareness is the Self in all beings, is the meaning of friendship.

This understanding, that the individual self and the expanded impersonal Self are in reality one and the same, is the dawning of the highest Peace. This Peace, present in the heart as Silence, is the uncreated Self.

TAPAS, WALKING THROUGH FIRE

In India, the word *Tapas* (austerity) is used as a synonym for all spiritual practices. Anyone walking the path is called a *Tapasvi*. *'Tapas'* comes from the word *'Taap'*, which literally means fire. The fire that burns away the conditioning and tendencies which are covering one's true nature. To come out of bondage, means to walk through fire. It is a way of saying how difficult this is. This is the fire, which burns away the noise that is covering the Silence.

Any practice is an exploration into the unknown, like a psychic adventure. When one takes a step in this direction, it will seem that all kinds of inner reactions start happening. One may feel an acute boredom, an intense desire to run to someone for company, or seek some form of distraction. One may feel overwhelmed by fear and confusion. Past memories that have been suppressed may come up very strongly, especially memories of pain and hurt. One may be amazed at how the entire past is sitting in one's mind in such clear detail. In extreme cases there may be physical reactions like headaches, body aches and nausea.

Then we understand why the practice is called *'Tapas'*. The fire represents the inner intensity that is needed to keep walking on the path. The fire also represents the purification process that reduces the barriers to ashes.

In fact, if the fire is not generated, there is no practice. It is like trying to cook in the kitchen without any heat. The fire blazes when the practice takes one to the edge of one's comfort zone. Even day-to-day events in life can create this fire of *Tapas*. For example, by not responding blindly to an insult, one may feel a burning in the body and it may become very uncomfortable. If one had responded mechanically, the burning sensation may not have been there.

Similarly, fasting for a day or two will create extreme discomfort, not so much because of the hunger, rather from the break in the habit pattern of eating. In the same way, becoming silent for a day, waking up early in the morning to practice, all can become *Tapas*. Addictions like smoking, drinking, shopping, watching television, all contain within them the possibility of awakening the fire of *Tapas*. Any action that is done mechanically and has become a habit, tends to stagnate one's natural flow of energy. Living spontaneously and non-mechanically becomes the *Tapas* that liberates the flow.

The body requires food three times a day, but if food is not given to the body, it does not collapse right away.

Why, because it is able to draw on the reserves, and may continue for a long time before dying. In the same way, the habitual mind requires food, not just three times a day but every moment.

That is why, most of us hear this non-stop dialogue in the head and have a need for continuous activity and interaction. When one starts to watch this dialogue, instead of reacting to it, the food that the mind needs is cut off. No new fuel is given. So the mind starts to draw on the reserves, in order to survive. The reserves are nothing but old memories, patterns and tendencies.

Whatever emotion, feeling, pain, trauma is present in these memories and patterns, will then come up, to be experienced. This willingness to consciously experience the discomfort instead of running away, is *Tapas*. This sounds easy but is the most difficult thing to do, because running away from pain, the fight or flight response, is a deeply ingrained pattern.

When one neither indulges nor resists, the energy locked up in the patterns has no place to go. It starts to get uncomfortable and the more energy locked in these patterns, the stronger the fire and the hotter it gets. Staying in this place, wide open, one faces whatever comes up. In practice, it takes up every ounce of ones inner strength, commitment and faith. One will feel that there is no way one can go through this. This reaching the limit is very important because this limit is the limit of the ego self. When this limit is reached and one does not escape, there is a break-through.

Ego is not destroyed. The heat of the practice melts the ego and this melting of the ego, is the arriving of love. The ego is nothing but Awareness congealed in a form. Like a candle made out of wax. The melting of the candle does not make the wax go away. It liberates the wax from the form of the candle. Then there is a feeling that one can go anywhere, do anything and that one can open up to anybody without hang-ups.

Now, Awareness starts to feel like a lamp of wisdom, that one can shine on anything. The deep nature of that thing will get revealed. The fire of *Tapas*, which in the beginning seemed as if it would destroy one, in time becomes a faithful companion.

In the world today, as the spiritual scene gets popular, there is a tendency not to talk about *Tapas*, as it might turn off potential customers. The advertisements for *Yoga* and spiritual retreats mostly talk about the good time that one will have and what one will gain. It becomes just another way to enjoy oneself and to be spiritually entertained. On the contrary, a beneficial practice must press our buttons, take us to the edge to release the poison. This is how purification happens.

From the point of view of *Chup Sadhana*, the greatest *Tapas* is the willingness to be alone and quiet without running away. This willingness to rest as Silence, reveals Silence as a tremendously creative state. The *Shakti* or power of this Silence is qualitatively different from the *Shakti* that one manifests as an individual.

बहूनां जन्मनामन्ते ज्ञानवान्मां प्रपद्यते ।
वासुदेवः सर्वमिति स महात्मा सुदुर्लभः ॥

Bahūnām janmanām ante jñānavān māṁ prapadyate
Vāsudevaḥ sarvam iti sa mah'ātmā sudurlabhaḥ

Bhagavad Gita ch 7 verse 19

The Self in the heart, which is birthless and deathless, imagining itself to be a person, experiences uncountable births and uncountable deaths. After repeated experiences of suffering, at some point, by the Grace of God, the inward journey begins. The inward journey leads one to the Tattva, the Source, the Self in the heart (Vasudeva), in which the seeker dissolves and only 'That' remains.

Such a Being, who has managed to turn away from the world of name and form and has found the Source in the heart, is indeed very rare.

TATTVA

In *Sanskrit*, the word *'Tat'* means 'That'. *'Tattva'* means 'Thatness'. It is a word used to denote that ground, that foundation on which everything is resting. It is the ground which is Indescribable, which is the reason why only the word 'That' is used. It is 'That', in which nothing has ever happened. The ground, the base, the support in which there are no opposites, yet, which is the basis of all the opposites.

It is described variously as *Tao, Dharma, Brahman*, etc. It is this ground, which is the Source and basis behind all religions, all sects, all philosophies but cannot be encompassed by any philosophy. Those who believe in God and those who deny God, both derive their certainty and their truth from this Source. Whatever name one invokes to worship the highest, one is only invoking this ground. Many religions consider it a blasphemy to give name and form to that Source and many religions consider it perfectly alright to worship that Source in different forms.

All the qualities attributed to 'That' are from the point of view of duality, because in 'That', there is no duality. People say that truth is 'One' to differentiate from 'many'. But in 'That' there is no 'One' and no 'many'. Some say God is great to differentiate from that which is not great. But in 'That', there is no 'great' and 'not great'. Similarly, the Highest is said to be light, to differentiate from darkness. In 'That', there is only that light in which both light and darkness are appearing. Some say that God is 'Now' or 'Present', as opposed to being in the past and future. But in 'That', there is no time in which these categories can exist.

Nobody and nothing can ever be separated from this *'Tattva'* even for a second. It was not possible in the past nor will it be possible in the future. Just like the existence of a wave can never be separated from the ocean. The ocean is the basis of all the waves, or the waves are nothing but the ocean.

Another example is that of gold and ornaments made out of gold. Ornaments maybe many but the gold that gives them value, is one. If the gold is taken out of the ornaments, there are no ornaments.

The same 26 letters of the alphabet become the greatest works of literature, mediocre fiction, religious books and sensational newspapers. The 26 letters remain unchanged and retain their intrinsic purity. They do not undergo the slightest modification. If one were to remove the alphabet, all the books ever written would disappear.

Similarly, the entire creation is nothing but the *'Tattva'*. It is said, that on knowing the *'Tattva'*, the Ground, the world disappears. Actually the world does not disappear rather the Source is seen as manifesting as the world. This is 'shifting'. Even the one seeing and what is being seen, then are not separate from the *'Tattva'*. The Source is seeing the Source, as the world.

Tattva is the impersonal Self, and also appears as each individual personality. On seeking one's Source, the *Tattva* is found and the illusion of separateness comes to an end. The individual seeker, who was just a bundle of likes and dislikes, based on deep-rooted beliefs, dissolves into this expansion. Even to say dissolves is not correct, because in 'That' there is no duality of personal and Impersonal. At this point, there is nobody left to even describe this state. That is why in the *Tao Te Ching,* it is said, 'those who know, don't talk and those who talk, don't know.' In the *Tattva*, the trinity of the Knower, the Known and the Knowing comes to an end. Who should describe which experience to whom, when there is only one undifferentiated Existence. The closest way to describe 'That' is Silence or peace. The peace 'that passeth understanding', means the peace which is not an opposite of disturbance. That Peace, in which both peace and war happen.

The search for the *Tattva* is unlike any other search in life. It is not the search for anything outside. It can be described as the pursuit of nothing, and therefore the true search must lead to a cessation of all searching. When all the searching has come to an end, what is left over, is Self as Silence.

The individual cannot know the *Tattva* because the individual is the only obstruction. When the individual drops, only the *Tattva* remains. An individual is also only the *Tattva* manifesting. Here, *Nirvana* and *Samsara* become the same. *Samsara* is the *Tattva* in action and *Nirvana* is the *Tattva* at rest. In the Silence, where one wants nothing, has nothing, knows nothing, resists nothing, what is present is the *Tattva* as Silence. *Islam*, which literally means surrender, is pointing to this Silence. When surrender has happened, one should become quiet.

This is what is meant by *Chup Sadhana*. One does not try to become quiet. In this state of cessation, stopping for short periods, one has glimpses of the Source.

The no-practice practice of *Chup Sadhana* develops the resulting Silence and effortlessness become habitual. The cravings and aversions, the patterns of accepting and rejecting, subside. The past and the future disappear in the 'Now'.

What remains is 'That'.

Printed in Great Britain
by Amazon